HEROES
OF WORLD WAR II

Stories of extreme bravery
in the face of battle

HEROES
OF WORLD WAR II
Stories of extreme bravery in the face of battle

ROBIN CROSS

CRESCENT BOOKS
New York

An Elephant Editions Book

© 1997 by Elephant Editions Limited

All rights reserved under International and Pan-American
Copyright Conventions.

. No part of this book may be reproduced or transmitted in any form
or by any means, electronic or mechanical including photocopying, recording
or by any information storage and retrieval system, without permission in
writing from the publisher and copyright holder.

This 1997 edition is published by Crescent Books,
a division of Random House Value Publishing, Inc.,
201 East 50th Street, New York, NY 10022.

Crescent Books and colophon are trademarks of
Random House Value Publishing, Inc.

Random House
New York • Toronto • London • Sydney • Auckland
http://www.randomhouse.com/

A CIP catalog record for this book is available from the Library of Congress

ISBN 1-517-184338-9

8 7 6 5 4 3 2 1

The Author
Robin Cross has written over 30 books, including
the No. 1 bestseller *We'll Meet Again* (with wartime
sweetheart Dame Vera Lynn), and the internationally recognized
VE-Day: Victory in Europe 1945. He was consultant editor for the
Guinness Encyclopedia of Warfare, and one of the principal
contributors to the Reader's Digest *World at War*.
He writes regularly on military matters for London's
The Daily Telegraph, and was one of the newspaper's
Gulf War reporting team. He has written over 30 television
documentaries, many of them on military and intelligence subjects.

Credits
Editor: Ray Bonds
Design direction: Robert Mathias, Publishing Workshop
Design : Helen Mathias
Photo research: Tony Moore
Typesetting and color reproduction: SX Composing DTP
Printed and bound in Spain by Book Print, S. L.

─────────────── **Jacket and front matter photos:** ───────────────

Jacket front:
MAIN PIC: Troops from an American landing
party give their buddies a helping hand when
their landing craft was sunk off Utah Beach,
D-Day, June 6 1944.
LEFT: Members of the US 503rd Parachute
Infantry Regiment jump to a field on
Corregidor, February 16 1945.
RIGHT: Marines move out from a Pacific
island beachhead onto a smoke-covered
airstrip held by the Japanese, November 23
1943.

Jacket back:
MAIN PIC: 10th Gurkha Rifles move past
caved-in bunkers after fierce fighting on
'Scraggy Hill' during the battle of Imphal-
Kohima, March-July 1944.
INSET TOP: A French Legionnaire proudly
displays his flag atop a truck after his unit's
epic battle to escape at Bir Hacheim, Western
Desert, June 1942.
INSET BOTTOM: HMS *Onslow* (in company with
HMS A*shanti*) ploughs through the waves; she
put up a tremendous fight during the Battle of
the Barents Sea, January 1943.

Front matter:
PAGE 1: Jim Rosenthal's famous picture of US
Marines raising the flag on Mount Suribachi
during the fight to re-take Iwo Jima, February
23 1945.
PAGE 3: Under heavy smoke and mortar fire
Fifth Army troops prepare to move forward
across rocky ground at Monastery Hill, Monte
Cassino, April 8 1944.
PAGE 5: A Royal Navy X-craft, with CO by the
conning tower, moves out to sea; six such
midget craft and their crews heroically set out
to attack the German battleship *Tirpitz* in
Norwegian waters, September 1943.

CONTENTS

The Flying Tigers 6

The Capture of Eben Emael 10

The Bruneval Raid 14

Boyington's Black Sheep 18

The Dam Busters 22

U-47 at Scapa Flow 26

The Rock Force at Corregidor 30

The French at Bir Hacheim 34

The Bridge at Remagen 38

PT-boats in the Pacific 42

US Rangers at Pointe du Hoc 46

The Nelson Touch 50

The Marines at Iwo Jima 54

The SAS, Northwest Europe 58

Gran Sasso Rescue 62

The Chindits Expeditions 66

The Epic of the X-craft 70

The Battle of Monte Cassino 74

The Marines at Wake Island 78

The Heroes of Kohima 82

Darby's Rangers in Tunisia 86

Swordfish at Taranto 90

The Cherkassy Break-out 94

The Taking of Pegasus Bridge 98

Wittmann's Tank Battles 102

The Doolittle Raid 106

Index 110

Picture credits 112

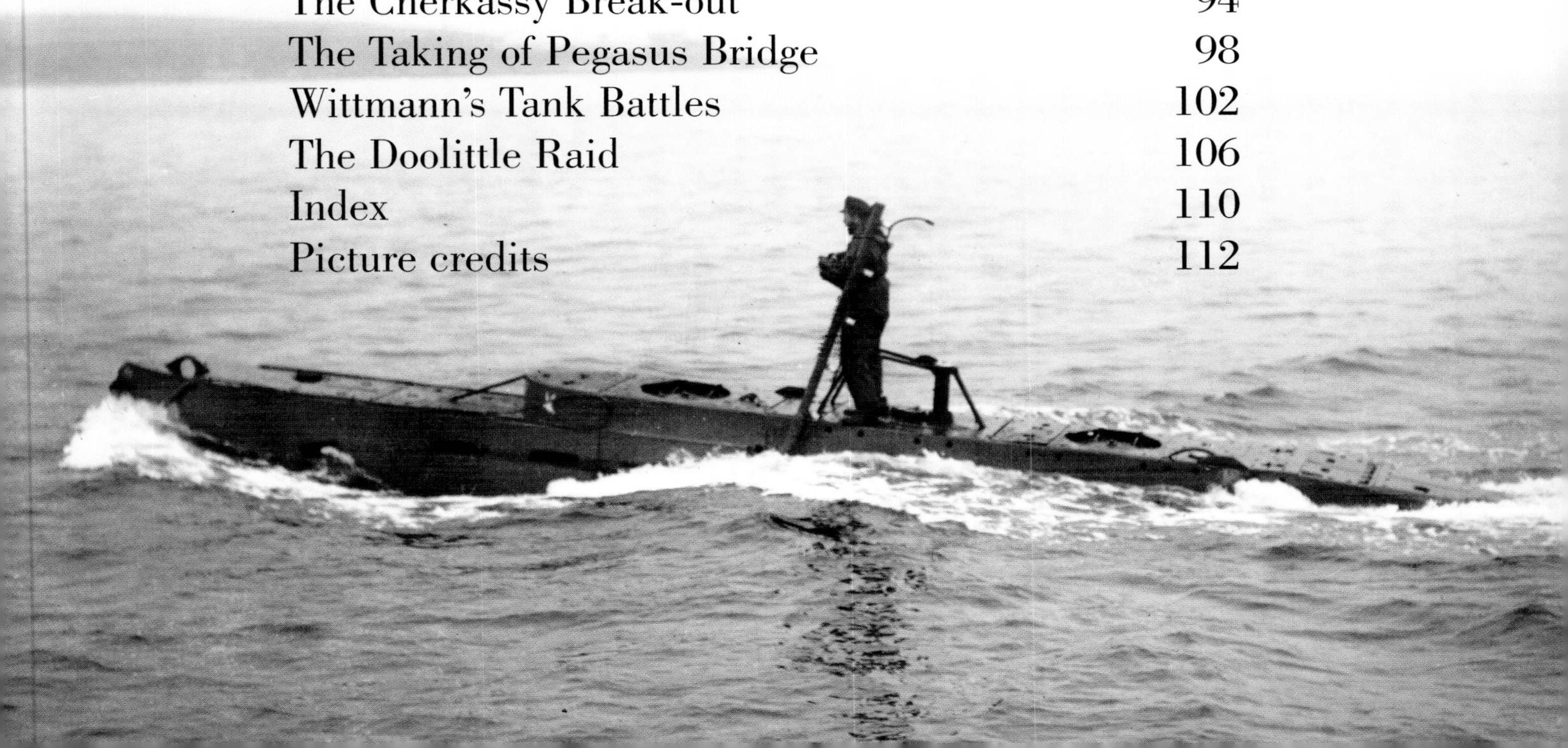

The Flying Tigers

ABOVE: Pilots of the Flying Tigers scramble for their P-40s. At the beginning of December 1941, their commander, Colonel Claire Chennault, could field only 62 aircraft against the might of the Japanese Air Force.

On December 20 1941, at an ice-bound airfield outside the city of Kunming in China's Yunnan province, were scattered some 50 American Curtiss P-40 Tomahawk fighters, marked with the blue and white star of China and a row of vicious-looking shark's teeth painted under their noses. In small wooden alert shacks nearby lounged three dozen Americans, pilots of the First and Second Squadrons of the American Volunteer Group in China (AVG), soon to become known as the Flying Tigers. Their commander was a stocky, taciturn, weatherbeaten American airman, Claire Chennault, who, as the aviation adviser to the leader of China's Kuomintang, Chiang Kai-shek, had been at war with the Japanese since 1937.

Chennault had retired from the Air Corps on April 30 1937, but within months he was waging combat in the undeclared war against Japan, which had invaded China, securing the entire coast and large tracts of the Chinese interior.

From the outset, the small, badly equipped and poorly trained Chinese Air Force was ill-prepared to offer effective resistance to the Japanese. Chennault masterminded the building of new airfields in outlying and less vulnerable areas, established a radio net to allow time to intercept Japanese bombing raids on previously defenceless cities, and introduced new tactics.

Within days of these tactics being implemented, 54 Japanese aircraft had been shot down. This swiftly brought an end to unescorted Japanese bombing missions. Chennault also flew lone combat missions in a Curtiss Hawk 75 Special which had been obtained for him by Madame Chiang Kai-shek. He is said to have shot down up to 40 Japanese aircraft on these patrols.

Now, however, the Japanese brought into service the Mitsubishi Zero. This machine, destined to be Japan's front-line fighter from 1940 to 1943, was a superb fighter despite a number of drawbacks. It was heavily armed with two 20mm cannon and two 7.7in machine guns. With a top speed of 300mph (480km/h), the Zero could cope with all opposition and its agility and rate of climb ensured its safety in combat. Chennault was to get to know the Zero very well in the coming years.

Chennault managed to stave off defeat with the infusion of Soviet pilots and aircraft following a non-aggression pact negotiated between China and the Soviet Union in the summer of 1937. But by the end of 1940 Soviet aid had been withdrawn. Chennault knew that China's survival now depended on American intervention but the United States' neutrality at this stage in the war posed obvious diplomatic problems. Nevertheless, by February 1941 discreet but persistent lobbying of the US government and military had secured their agreement to the formation of an American aerial 'foreign legion' whose men – 190 ground personnel and 109 former Army, Navy and Marine Corps pilots – would be employed by a private company, the Central Aircraft Manufacturing Company (CAMCO). In June 1941 the first AVG group set sail from San Francisco.

The aircraft they were to fly was the Curtiss-Wright P-40 Tomahawk, by no means one of the great fighters of the war but rugged and dependable. It had self-sealing fuel tanks and packed a punch with two wing-mounted .303 machine-guns and a pair of synchronised 0.5in guns firing through the propeller. With its great weight of armour and guns, the Tomahawk could outdive the Zero, but it struggled in a dogfight with its nimble Japanese adversary.

The AVG's first base was at Toungoo, in Burma, a hard-surfaced airfield in the sweltering, malarial jungle north of Rangoon which had been leased to China by Britain's Royal Air Force on the condition that it be used for training purposes only.

Chennault relished the freedom of action he enjoyed in welding a disparate group of pilots – some of whom had never flown a fighter – into an effective combat formation. He drilled them in the assets of the Tomahawk – its diving speed and firepower – and taught them to avoid dogfights with the more manoeuvrable Japanese A6M Zero, which had first appeared over China in 1940. He also placed great emphasis on gunnery.

As war between Japan and the United States approached, Chennault was still working the Flying Tigers up to strength. At the beginning of December 1941 he had only 82 pilots and 62 aircraft in commission. On December 7 Japanese carrier-borne aircraft attacked the US naval base at Pearl Harbor in Hawaii. The following day the United States declared war on Japan.

Although he was eager to move the AVG into Yunnan, the better to protect the Burma Road, China's supply lifeline, Chennault was at first

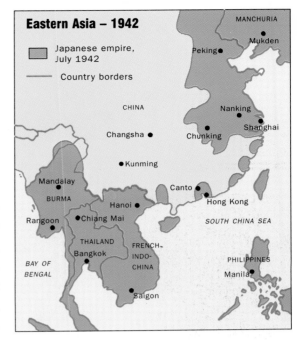

Eastern Asia – 1942

Japanese empire, July 1942

—— Country borders

MANCHURIA
Mukden
Peking
CHINA
Nanking
Changsha
Chunking
Shanghai
Kunming
Mandalay
Canton
BURMA
Hanoi
Hong Kong
Rangoon
Chiang Mai
SOUTH CHINA SEA
THAILAND
FRENCH INDO-CHINA
Bangkok
PHILIPPINES
BAY OF BENGAL
Manila
Saigon

BELOW: The legendary 'shark's teeth' nose of the Tigers' Tomahawks. A similar device had already been used by a British Eighth Air Force fighter squadron in the Western Desert. but the Tigers made it their own.

ordered to remain at Toungoo and co-operate with the RAF. On December 15 he was ordered to maintain one squadron at Rangoon and move the other two to Kunming, the northern terminus of the Burma Road, 5,000ft (1,500m) up on the great plateau of Yunnan. The pattern was to hold for the desperate months which were to follow – a rotation of squadrons between Mingladon base and its satellite fields at Rangoon and Chennault's headquarters at Kunming. Initially, the AVG's Third Squadron was held back at Rangoon.

The AVG swung into action on December 20 1941. The monsoon season was over and Japanese bombers were once more flying against Kunming. Ten of them were intercepted over the city by the Flying Tigers, who downed six of them without losing any of their pilots. The action dealt a severe psychological blow to the Japanese, who had previously flown unhindered over Kunming.

Three days later Third Squadron fought their first action against heavy odds. Fifty-four Japanese bombers, flying from the air base at Bangkok and escorted by 20 fighters, including eight Zeros, were met by 14 Flying Tiger Tomahawks and 23 of the RAF's stubby, obsolete Buffalo fighters. Between them, they claimed 32 Japanese aircraft shot down for combined losses of seven pilots and 14 planes. The AVG's Bob 'Duke' Hedman and R. T. 'Tadpole' Smith both claimed five kills to share honours as the first American pilots to become aces in a single encounter. Hedman had pursued the enemy bombers out into the Gulf of Siam and landed with only five gallons (23 litres) of fuel in his tank, his Tomahawk a sieve of bullet holes and its ammunition spent.

Over Christmas there was a bitter fight for air superiority over Rangoon. When sheer weight of numbers failed to sweep the Flying Tigers from the sky, the Japanese attempted to lure them up with nuisance raids while large formations of their fighters lurked high in the sun. Japanese bombers raided Mingladon and fighters slashed over the field, strafing everything in their sights. The AVG's mechanics built dozens of dummy aircraft, stuffed with combustible rice straw, and lined them up on the runway to draw the ground attackers away from the real Tomahawks dispersed under mango and banyan trees on the edge of the airfield.

The AVG's success over Rangoon forced the Japanese to abandon daylight raids for night bombing. But tactical success was achieved against a background of strategic defeat as the Japanese extended their control of the Pacific islands, invaded lower Burma, and by the beginning of March 1942 were threatening Rangoon.

Chennault's Flying Tigers now faced another threat, that of induction into the United States Army Air Force (USAAF), as Washington moved to bring the unit back under the American flag. Chennault resisted, fearing that if the AVG became a regular US Army task force its identity and tactical flexibility would disappear under a blizzard of red tape. Above all, Chennault believed that a small but effective air force, free to strike at the most advantageous time and place, could exercise an influence out of all proportion to its paper strength.

Rangoon was abandoned on March 6. Thanks to the efforts of the AVG – on February 25 alone it had accounted for 22 Japanese fighters and a single bomber – the evacuation from Rangoon was free of Japanese air attack. At the beginning of March, with the arrival of Lieutenant-General Joseph Stilwell, the US commander in China, Chennault opened hostilities on a third front. 'Vinegar Joe', a China expert, was also an infantryman through and through, and his appointment inevitably provoked a bitter and long-running dispute about the relative priorities given to ground and air operations.

After the fall of Rangoon, the AVG moved to Magwe, then Loiwing. Husbanding their dwindling resources, and migrating from airfield to airfield, they avoided pitched air battles and concentrated on ground attack raids on Japanese airstrips. Japanese anti-aircraft fire was always ferocious.

In April 1942, Chennault was recalled to active duty in the USAAF with the rank of Brigadier-General and placed in command of the China Air Task Force, the AVG in all but name, consisting of 34 Tomahawks and seven B-25 bombers. The formal induction of the AVG into the USAAF took place on July 10. In March 1943 the China Air Task Force was redesignated the 14th Air Force, functioning independently from the USAAF under the command of Chennault, now with the rank of Major-General and still at loggerheads with Stilwell over the role of air power.

Meanwhile, the Flying Tigers fought a desperate battle for survival on the disintegrating Burma front. At the beginning of May its pilots flew repeated bombing and strafing missions against Japanese forces probing up the Burma Road. When a Japanese column attempted to bridge the spectacular, plunging Salween Gorge, the last natural obstacle between Burma and China, the AVG redoubled its efforts.

Regret at the passing of the AVG was tempered by its remarkable record. The Flying Tigers had officially destroyed 297 enemy aircraft, losing only 14 of their own planes in combat. Their determined resistance over Rangoon had ensured the orderly evacuation of the city. And they had played a vital role in halting the Japanese advance up the Burma Road at Salween. Sadly, they could not save the Road itself, which the Japanese closed by the end of February.

All this was achieved at a remarkably low cost: four men taken prisoner and 22 dead (four in combat, five in strafing raids, three killed by bombs and ten in crashes).

ABOVE: Chennault keeping a close eye on running repairs at Kunming. An heroic but fiery character, Chennault resigned from the command of 14th Air Force in 1945 after his advice on the reorganisation of the Chinese Air Force was ignored.

The Capture of Eben Emael

ABOVE: The forbidding northeast face of the supposedly impregnable stronghold of Eben Emael, photographed after its daring capture.

BELOW: Grime-caked and triumphant, paratroops of Assault Section Granite relax after the completion of their mission.

On May 10 1940 Adolf Hitler launched his Blitzkrieg against France and the Low Countries. The single most striking episode on that momentous day was the capture by German airborne troops of the Belgian fortress at Eben Emael.

Completed in 1935, the fortress guarded the vital bridges at the confluences of the Albert Canal and the Maas River. Its speedy capture was crucial to Hitler's entire plan of pinning the French and British in the north while delivering his main blow to the south, driving through the Ardennes to outflank the French defensive system of the Maginot Line.

Eben Emael was more formidable than anything in the Maginot Line. The Belgian high command considered it impregnable, protected on its northeast face by a cutting which dropped 120ft (37m) sheer into the Albert Canal. Eben Emael's heavily armoured single and double turrets mounted two 120mm guns and six 75mm guns and its approaches were covered by anti-tank and machine-guns. Eben Emael bristled with no fewer than 64 strongpoints, built on different levels and thought to be impervious to all but the most violent and prolonged artillery bombardment.

Minefields and barbed wire entanglements were sited to channel attackers into killing grounds, and the fortress's command post and barracks, the latter big enough to hold a garrison of 1,200 men, were buried underground. However, like all fixed defences, Eben Emael had a weakness – it had very few anti-aircraft weapons and the surface of the fort was unmined.

Adolf Hitler had grasped this when he informed Major-General Kurt Student, commanding the 7th Airborne Division, 'The top is like a meadow, gliders can land on it.' Thus were the seeds laid for the airborne assault on Eben Emael.

The task of capturing the fortress was given to the paratroop engineers of Assault Section Granite, part of a larger formation, Assault Group Koch, which was tasked with the seizing of the bridges over the Albert Canal.

Training for the operation began at Hildesheim under conditions of great secrecy in November 1939. Leave was forbidden, as was fraternisation with men from other units. Many of the men did not even know the name of their target until after its capture. But scale models and field exercises against the bunkers of Czech fortreseses in the Sudetenland made them familiar with Eben Emael's every nook and cranny.

At 3.30am on May 10, Assault Group Granite took off from the Cologne-Ostheim airfield in 11 big DFS 230 gliders towed by Ju52 tugs. The paratroops were armed to teeth, but the most important weapons they took them were the 48 shaped charges specially designed to punch holes in Eben Emael's armour.

On the journey to Eben Emael. The assault group lost two of its gliders when their tow ropes snapped. One of them was carrying Granite's commander, Lieutenant Rudolf Witzig. He came down in

The capture of Eben Emael
May 10 1940

Maas

Juliana Canal

Albert Canal

Veldwezelt

Maastricht

BELGIUM

HOLLAND

Vroenhaven

Kanne

Eben Emael

Fort
Eben
Emael

Albert Canal

Maas

German airborne
assaults

a field near Cologne, where he immediately called up another Ju52 to tow him off.

The remaining nine gliders flew on, dropping dummy parachutists filled with firecrackers to confuse the Belgian defenders. At Aachen the gliders were cast off at a height of 8,000ft (2,440m) to glide silently down on Eben Emael like great birds of prey.

They arrived on top of their target at 5.20am, taking the fortress's 700 defenders completely by surprise. Two gliders had difficult landings which prevented their paratroops from taking an effective part in the battle, but the remaining seven disgorged 55 men of Assault Group Granite, now under the command of Sergeant-Major Helmut Wenzel, straight into action.

One by one the the engineers used their shaped charges to blast the thick steel cupolas which protected Eben Emael's guns, driving their crews into the labyrinth of tunnels below. The armour of the twin 120mm turret proved too much even for the devastating charges. It was eventually blown up by the simple expedient of stuffing explosive charges down the barrels.

The commander of Eben Emael. Major Jottrand, seemed paralysed. Isolated in his command post, deep below ground, and buffeted by the successive shocks of the charges exploding above, he had no idea of the strength of the forces attacking him and was bewildered by the rapid loss of so many of his strongpoints. He called up artillery fire from nearby field batteries, but this failed to dislodge the Germans from the fortress's glacis.

About three hours after the battle had begun, Witzig's lone glider flew into Eben Emael. He ordered his men into the fort to clean out its demoralised defenders. Meanwhile other glider-borne units of Assault Group Koch had secured two nearby bridges over the Albert Canal.

Night fell. Later Witzig recalled: 'After the hard fighting of the day, the detachment lay exhausted and parched, under scattered fire from the Belgian artillery and infantry outside the fortification; every burst of fire might have signalled the beginning of the counter-attack we expected and our nerves were tense. For the most part, however, the enemy lacked the will to fight.'

Assault Group Granite was relieved the following morning by a detachment of engineers and infantry of Sixth Army. At around 1pm the Belgians ran up a white flag. The impregnable fortress of

ABOVE AND BACKGROUND: Paratroop training. General Kurt Student's fledgling 7th Airborne Division was not ready to participate in the early stages of the Second World War and first saw action in the Norway campaign in April 1940 where it distinguished itself in the relief of Narvik.

ABOVE: The devastating effect of hollow charges on one of Eben Emael's strongpoints.

LEFT: A DFS 230 glider, capable of carrying 600lb (272kg) of freight in addition to troops. When released from a height of 6,500ft (2,000m) it could glide for 12 miles (20km), but remained vulnerable to ground fire during its long, shallow approach to landing. Later variants were fitted with a tail-mounted machine-gun for suppressive fire.

Eben Emael had fallen, its garrison defeated by fewer than 100 paratroops. In the fighting Witzig had lost six men killed and 20 wounded. it was a tribute to the meticulous planning of the operation and the quality of the trops who carried it out.

Hitler expressed his personal satisfaction with Witzig's daring *coup de main*, and the commander of Assault Group Granite was awarded the Knight's Cross and promoted to the rank of captain. Within 30 hours the Germans had breached the line of Albert Canal and fatally undermined Allied plans for meeting a German attack. Even more important, perhaps, was the psychological blow dealt by the sudden collapse of Eben Emael in one of the most brilliant airborne operations of the war.

The Bruneval Raid

BACKGROUND AND DETAIL (RIGHT): An aerial reconnaissance photograph of the Wurzburg radar at Bruneval, taken on December 5 1941 by a Spitfire flown by Squadron Leader A.E. Hill.

RIGHT: After the raid Squadron Leader Pickard chats with the men his Whitley bombers had dropped in France only a few hours earlier.

In February 1942, the men of the newly formed British 1st Airborne Division went into action for the first time. In one of the most daring raids of the war, they seized and brought back to England vital components of a German 'Wurzburg' radar installation.

Radar was one of the key high-technology battlegrounds of the war. It had secured RAF Fighter Command its narrow margin of victory in the Battle of Britain. In the Blitz, the Luftwaffe had used radio navigation aids as blind bombing devices, precipitating the so-called 'battle of the beams' as the British strove to jam them.

In 1941 British bombers began to take the war to the heart of Germany, forcing the Luftwaffe to develop its own defensive radars. Keeping a close track on German technical developments, and devising counters to them, was Dr. R.V. Jones of the Air Staff.

Throughout 1941, Jones and his team built up a detailed picture of the German radar network on the Channel coast. That autumn, a series of low-level photo-reconnaissance pictures revealed the presence of a newly installed Wurzburg early warning radar on a clifftop at Bruneval, a village near the French port of Le Havre.

Below the installation lay a beach, and Jones was immediately struck by the idea of despatching a commando raid to retrieve the Wurzburg array from its exposed position. The idea was passed from Air Intelligence to the headquarters of Combined Operations whose chief, Lord Louis Mountbatten, approved the plan.

First the German defences at Bruneval were reconnoitred by the French Resistance. Back in England, it was decided that a frontal assault on the beach would meet heavy resistance. The mission would be undertaken by paratroops dropped inland by Whitley bombers of the RAF under the command of Squadron Leader Charles Pickard. After completing the operation, they would be taken off the beach by the Royal Navy.

The unit chosen for the operation was C Company of the 2nd Battalion of the 1st Parachute Brigade, 120 men commanded by Major John Frost. Nearly all the men were drawn from Scottish regiments, including the Black Watch, Cameron Highlanders, King's Own Scottish Borderers and Seaforths. They were to be accompanied by a technical expert, an RAF radar operator, Flight Sergeant C.W.H. Cox, whose job it would be to dismantle the Wurzburg. Cox, a former cinema projectionist, had never been in a ship or an aircraft before.

The plan for the operation was simple. The paratroops were to be dropped in three bodies. The first, under the leadership of Lieutenant John Ross and Lieutenant Euen Charteris, was to advance on and capture the beach. The second, subdivided into three sections and commanded by Frost, was to seize the villa and the Wurzburg. The third, led by Lieutenant John Timothy was to act as a rearguard and reserve.

The raiding party was ready for action by February 20 1942. Training had revolved around a scale model made by the RAF's Photographic Interpretation Unit and full-scale exercises on the south coast.

GREAT BRITAIN

Thruxton

Portsmouth

ENGLISH CHANNEL

Cherbourg

Bruneval

le Havre

FRANCE

ABOVE: A trouble-free evacuation from the beach was considered vital to the success of the Bruneval raid and men and landing craft were put through their paces during training.

BELOW: The Armstrong Whitworth Whitley, the first British bomber to fly over Berlin. Designed in 1934, it was obsolete by 1942 but did sterling service as a trainer, anti-submarine aircraft, paratroop training transport and glider tug

FAR RIGHT: Mission accomplsihed. The return of the Bruneval raiders. Major Frost can be seen (helmeted with moustache) on the bridge.

After several anxious days of waiting for the weather to clear the raid went in on the night of February 27/28. The Whitleys dropped the paratroops from a height of 600ft (180m) on to the countryside below.

Lieutenant Charteris's two sections were dropped about a mile and a half (2.5km) beyond their intended position. Charteris quickly regained his bearings and his men set off across the icy landscape at the double.

Frost's section took only ten minutes to gather at their rendezvous point. They met no oposition as they moved on the villa, Flight Sergeant Cox and an engineer detachment hauling trolleys over a succession of barbed wire obstacles. Frost's men surrounded the villa and, advancing towards the open front door, Frost blew his whistle.

Frost later recalled, 'Immediately, explosions, yells and the sound of automatic fire came from the proximity of the radar set.' The paratroops rushed the villa, which they found completely empty save for a single German firing from the top floor.

Soon afterwards Cox and the engineers began to get to grips with the Wurzburg, ripping most of its parts away by sheer force as bullets whistled around their ears. By now heavy fire from German positions in a wooded enclosure about 300 yards (275m) to the north of the villa was making life increasingly uncomfortable for Cox and the paras. The arrival of vehicles threatened an imminent mortar barrage, and after half an hour Frost gave the order to withdraw.

A machine-gun in a pillbox now barred the way to the beach, which was still held by the Gerrmans, who were also regrouping and advancing from the villa. At last, Charteris's two sections arrived, having already had a brisk encounter with an enemy patrol. The pillbox was silenced and the beach taken.

It was now about 2.15am, but the raiders were not out of the woods yet. There was no sign of the Royal Navy. Frost's signallers failed to make contact with the landing craft which were to evacuate the paras and, as a last resort, several red Verey lights were fired. Then, just as Frost was preparing to rearrange his defences to meet the anticipated German counterattack, one of his signallers shouted, 'Sir, the boats are coming in! The boats are here! God bless the ruddy navy, sir!'

The evacuation into six landing craft, with the sea running high and the Germans firing from the cliffs, was anything but orderly.

Two of Frost's signallers got lost and were left behind.

The raiders and their precious Wurzburg cargo were transferred to gunboats, where they learned that the Navy had been delayed by the presence in the area of a German destroyer and two E-boats. They German warships had passed within a mile (1.6km) of the landing craft but had not spotted them.

ABOVE: Cheers for the raiders from the flotilla of escort vessels welcoming them home.

As dawn came up, Royal Navy destroyers and a squadron of Spitfires arived to escort the flotilla to Portsmouth. The destroyers played 'Rule Britannia' over their loudhailers.

Two men had been killed in the operation and six were missing, all of whom survived the war. Two prisoners were brought back, one of them the Wurzburg's operator. The German report on the raid commented: 'The operation of the British commandos was well planned and was executed with great discipline . . . although attacked by German soldiers, they concentrated on their primary task'.

Boyington's Black Sheep

ABOVE: Vought F4U Corsairs warm up on a Bougainville landing strip. The Corsair was one of the powerful American fighters which broke the back of the Japanese Air Force in the Pacific.

On August 7 1942, US Marines had stormed ashore at Guadalcanal in the Solomons Chain, the first move in the American plan to isolate the massive Japanese base at Rabaul. It was not until November 1942, after a series of savage land, sea and air battles, that the fate of the Japanese on Guadalcanal was sealed. Nevertheless, the Japanese continued to maintain a substantial air presence in the region, estimated at about 400 aircraft. Their defeat was the task of Major-General Ralph J. Mitchell, who commanded a mixed force of fighters, bombers and support aircraft drawn from the USAAF, US Navy, US Marine Corps and Royal New Zealand Air Force.

One of the outstanding units in Mitchell's command was Marine Fighter Squadron 214 (VMF-214), led by Major Gregory Boyington, an extremely tough customer who had joined the US Marine Corps in in 1935 and had served under General Chennault in China in the American Volunteer Group, universally known as the Flying Tigers. Boyington had returned to the United States in July 1942 with six kills under his belt and rejoined the Marines. In September 1943, he was appointed commander of VMF-214, a unit which had previously fought in the Solomons but had been dispersed after its second tour of operations and existed only on

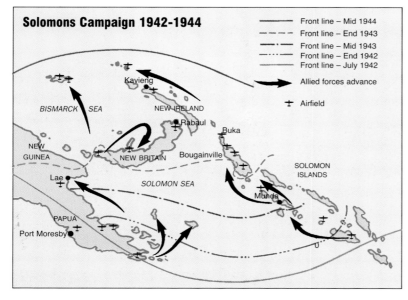

Solomons Campaign 1942-1944

Front line – Mid 1944
Front line – End 1943
Front line – Mid 1943
Front line – End 1942
Front line – July 1942
→ Allied forces advance
✛ Airfield

BISMARCK SEA
Kavieng
NEW IRELAND
Rabaul
Buka
NEW GUINEA
NEW BRITAIN
Bougainville
SOLOMON SEA
SOLOMON ISLANDS
Lae
Munda
PAPUA
Port Moresby

paper. Boyington was soon to breathe new life into the squadron whose interrupted existence earned it the nickname of 'The Black Sheep'.

At 30, Boyington was a highly experienced fighter pilot and, although he was not the oldest man in the squadron, he was dubbed 'Pappy'. A number of the Black Sheep were already veterans and, like the Flying Tigers before them, affected a studiously scruffy approach to their appearance. Boyington was a shrewd and sometimes controversial tactician. He once told a colleague that he did not expect his wingman to follow him into a fight, believing that he should take care of himself. Boyington quickly added that in a fight against superior odds a wingman was the best form of life insurance!

The fighter they flew was the formidable gull-winged F4U Corsair, which had been initially rejected as a carrier-based aircraft by the US Navy because of its long nose, which restricted visibility, and unreliable undercarriage. The Marines, however, had no inhibitions about the Corsair, and from the moment it entered combat in the Solomons in February 1943 the Corsair displayed a marked superiority to Japanese fighters. By the end of the war in the Pacific, the Corsair had accounted for 2,140 enemy aircraft.

Living conditions in the combat zone were exceptionally uncomfortable. The tents in which the pilots slept were marooned in seas of mud. They were attacked with equal regularity by malaria-carrying mosquitos and Japanese night bombers. Another enemy was the vile food they were obliged to eat; the men were as likely to be felled by dysentery as by enemy machine-gun bullets.

After a brief spell in the Russell Islands, VMF-214 moved to an airfield at Munda, on New Georgia Island. The Black Sheep made their operational debut on September 16 1943, flying escort to Ballale and claiming 11 downed Zeros out of an attacking force of 40, plus eight probables. Boyington claimed five, including one which blew up at close range, forcing him to fly through a curtain of debris. Boyington downed a second in a vain attempt to save one of his comrades, Captain Robert T. Ewing, who did not return from the mission.

The Black Sheep prospered in the Bougainville area. In their first month, they claimed 47 aircraft shot down. At the beginning of October, Boyington encountered an ingenious Japanese ruse. Leading the squadron over the enemy airfield at Kahili, he received a radio request to report his height and direction. The ground controller spoke in perfect English, but Boyington suspected that he was, in fact, Japanese. Boyington responded by revealing his true position but

BELOW: Sporting baseball caps donated by the St Louis Cardinals – one cap for every enemy plane downed – the men of VMF-214 pose for the cameras.

ABOVE: Ground crew gather round a battered Corsair after a raid on Rabaul, its tail surfaces torn by Zero machine-gun fire.

not the correct height – 20,000ft (6,000m) instead of the 25,000ft (7,600m) at which he was flying. Boyington's counter-deception worked. It was not long before he saw a formation of about 30 Zeros climbing beneath him. The Black Sheep attacked from out of the sun and in the space of 30 seconds Boyington claimed three more victims.

Larger and more prolonged air battles assumed an epic scale worthy of a Hollywood movie. Later, Boyington recalled: 'You could see the planes going around in circles, half-circles, you could see Zeros, Corsairs, Zeros, all firing at each other, you could see the red balls from the tracers, just like Roman candles going every which way in the sky. The battles would cover an area from about 300ft (90m) above the water to about 20,000ft (6,000m) and equally as wide.'

October 1943 found the Black Sheep stationed on the forward base at Vella Lavella, readying themselves for the air assault on Rabaul. However, Boyington's first sweep over the Japanese base was not an unqualified success. On December 17, General Mitchell put up 76 fighters drawn from Marine Corps and Navy squadrons and two squadrons of the Royal New Zealand Air Force. Boyington realised that a formation this size, containing aircraft with differing performances (Corsairs, Hellcats and Kittyhawks) was almost impossible to co-ordinate in the air.

Boyington introduced smaller sweeps of 35-50 aircraft of the same type. He was rewarded on December 23 when 48 Corsairs flew in immediately after an escorted bombing raid on Rabaul. The

Marine pilots encountered 40 Japanese fighters miling around and shot down 30 of them. The Black Sheep's share was 12, of which Boyington claimed five.

Boyington and his men went for a dozen Zeros which immediately ran for Rabaul, a sign that they were low on fuel. In all probability the Japanese pilots mistook the Black Sheep for escort planes, under orders to stay with the bombers, and thus did not expect to be pursued. Boyington singled out one of the Zeros and steadily closed the distance between them until he was only 50ft (15m) behind and dead on his tail. One short burst accounted for the unsuspecting Zero pilot, who baled out from his blazing aircraft. Boyington coolly watched as he hit the water.

Boyington then climbed until he spotted two more Zeros streaking towards Rabaul, one of them trailing smoke. Again, one burst was enough to account for the crippled Zero, whose pilot also baled out. The second Zero tried to get on Boyington's tail but the Marine ace put his nose down and dived away. This was the essence of air fighting at this stage in the war in the Pacific — well-thought-out and executed tactics, the coldblooded selection of targets and calculation of risk, combined with top-class gunnery and a superior aircraft. It spelled the end for Japanese air power.

From the Battle of Britain onwards, overclaiming was endemic among fighter pilots on all sides in World War II. Between mid-December 1943 and the beginning of January 1944, American pilots claimed to have shot down 147 enemy aircraft over Rabaul. However, Japanese records suggest that the real total was about 70. In spite of the overclaiming, it was enough to establish American air superiority.

Boyington was officially credited with 26 victories, but on January 3 – just five days before the squadron's tour of duty came to an end – he was shot down and made a prisoner-of -war. In common with all those who fell into Japanese hands, Boyington endured great hardship. But he survived to collect the Medal of Honor he had been awarded in April 1944 – remarkably, the very first decoration he had received from his country. Boyington was subsequently awarded the Navy Cross and finished the war as the top-scoring Marine ace, retiring with the rank of Colonel.

The Black Sheep re-entered combat in March 1945, flying against the coast of Japan from the carrier USS *Franklin*. They were a rookie outfit now, more like lambs than Boyington's grizzled veterans. This time, they were in action for only two days before *Franklin* sustained such heavy bomb damage that she was withdrawn from the theatre. Nevertheless, at the time of the Japanese surrender the Black Sheep were the seventh highest scoring Marine squadron, with 127 confirmed victories, the overwhelming majority gained under Boyington's leadership.

VMF-214 went on to perform sterling service during the Korean War and in Vietnam, moving on from their Corsairs to A-4 Skyhawks.

ABOVE: 'Pappy' Boyington briefs his pilots before a mission. His victory tally of six kills with the Flying Tigers and 22 with his Black Sheep, made Boyington the highest-scoring Marine ace of the war.

BACKGROUND PIC: Corsairs take off from the Cape Torokina airstrip on Bougainville. The immensely powerful and rugged Corsair had a maximum speed of 415mph (665km/h) at 20,000ft (6,000m) and a range of just over 1,000 miles (1,600km). Corsairs accounted for 2,140 enemy aircraft during the war, with a kill ratio of 11:1. It was also a formidable divebomber, and remained in production until 1952.

The Dam Busters

The pilots and aircrew who were brought together in 1943 by RAF Bomber Command to form 617 Squadron had a single aim – a daring attack on the heart of German war industry using an untried weapon, the so-called 'bouncing bomb'.

By early 1943, Bomber Command's strategic night offensive against Germany was stepping up a gear, aided by the arrival in numbers of four-engined Lancaster bombers equipped with increasingly sophisticated radio-navigation aids. Nevertheless, most of Bomber Command's effort went into the 'area bombing' of Germany's industrial cities rather than attacks on pinpoint targets.

However, there was a set of precise targets which Bomber Command had identified as vital to the German war effort – the reservoirs which supplied the industrial region of the Ruhr with much of its water and electricity, in particular those contained by the Eder and Moehne dams.

Although the chief of Bomber Command, Air Marshal Arthur Harris, remained sceptical about his bombers' ability to breach the dams, a special squadron – officially called Squadron X but soon designated 617 – was formed in mid-March 1943 to carry out attack on the dams. The weapon they were to use was also extremely special – the 'bouncing bomb' designed by the brilliant engineer Barnes Wallis (see page 25).

The squadron was commanded by one of the great airmen of the war, Wing Commander Guy Gibson. Although he was only 24 years old, the much-decorated Gibson was one of Bomber Command's most experienced pilots, a meticulous planner and natural leader of men. The 133 men of 617 Squadron who gathered at RAF Scampton, in Lincolnshire, were a mixed bunch, ranging from brilliant veterans like the extrovert Australian low-flying expert Mickey Martin to relative novices who had flown only a few operations.

But all of them had one thing in common. They had been specially selected by Gibson as

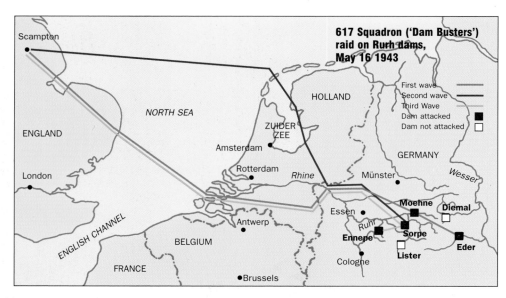

617 Squadron ('Dam Busters') raid on Ruhr dams, May 16 1943

First wave
Second wave
Third Wave
Dam attacked ■
Dam not attacked □

men who possessed the 'right stuff' for the operation, whose targets were still a secret. When they arrived at Scampton, however, the men of 617 Squadron noticed that their Lancasters's bomb bays had been heavily modified. Among their number were 29 Canadians, 12 Australians, 2 New Zealanders and an American, Flight Lieutenant Joe McCarthy.

The training that followed involved a punishing routine of low-level flying and bombing exercises. Precision was of the essence. Gibson had been informed by Barnes Wallis that the attack would have to be made over water at a height of 150ft (45m) – a figure later revised down to 60ft (20m) – and the bombs released precisely 1,275ft (389m) from the target.

The judging of the height over water on the bombing run was solved by fitting two angled spotlights to the nose and rear fuselage of each Lancaster. Their beams were designed to coincide on

ABOVE: Artist Frank Wootten's dramatic depiction of the 617 Squadron Lancaster raid on the Ruhr dams.

BELOW: The smashed Moehne dam several days after the raid, with over 150 yards (137m) of its masonry torn away and water still pouring through the breach.

the surface of the reservoir when the aircraft was at the correct height. The bomb aimer was given a simple V-shaped wooden device to judge the point of release. When the two nails at the ends of its arms coincided with the towers on the end of the dam, the bomb was dropped.

Meanwhile, Barnes Wallis and his team were working frantically to perfect the design of the bomb. Between May 11 and 14, at Reculver, 617 Squadron used full-sized practice bombs to attack canvas towers on the promenade. On the 15th Gibson was told that the attack – codenamed Operation Chastise – would be mounted on Sunday May 16.

Six target dams had been chosen. Gibson was to lead the main contingent, consisting of three formations of three aircraft, to attack the Moehne dam, then the Eder and, if any bombs were left, the Sorpe. The second wave of five aircraft, flying singly, would attack the Sorpe. The final five aircraft were to fly as a reserve, taking off two hours after the first wave, to be directed against any of the main targets or three other dams, the Lister, Diemel and Ennepe. To evade German air defences, the Lancasters were to fly under 500ft (150m) throughout the mission.

Led by Gibson, the first wave took off from Scampton just after 8.30pm. As they flew into the Ruhr at tree-top height, a power cable accounted for one of his Lancasters.

Gibson was the first to attack the Moehne shortly after midnight. Flying through heavy anti-aircraft fire, he dropped his bomb slightly off target; it burst on the reservoir bank just to the left of the huge dam. He was followed in by the second Lancaster, which got its bomb off too late. It overshot the dam but wrecked the power station beyond. Badly damaged by flak, the crippled Lancaster flew on for another 3 miles (5km) before exploding in a sheet of flame Its pilot, Flight Lieutenant Hopgood, had predicted that he would not survive the mission.

The third bomb missed the Moehne, but the fourth and fifth breached the dam, raising huge spouts of water against the moon. Water began to pour through the dam. To Gibson, circling the target, the floodwaters released by the bomb looked like 'stirred porridge' in the moonlight. Gibson transmitted the codeword for success, 'Nigger', named after his beloved black labrador, which had tragically been run over earlier in the day. He then led the remaining three aircraft with bombs to the Eder,

TOP: Post-strike reconnaissance photo of the Eder dam, which was not fully repaired until late in 1943.

ABOVE: Wing Commander Guy Gibson (top of steps) and his crew prepare to take off. Gibson was one of the great air leaders of the war, an inspirational airman who led from the front. He died in September 1944 when the Mosquito he was flying as a Master Bomber crashed in Holland. He had flown a total of 177 operational sorties, 76 of them as a bomber pilot, the rest in fighters.

while the others headed for home.

At the Eder, shrouded in early morning mist, the first two bombs failed to break the dam, but the third punched a gaping hole in it. A tidal wave of water poured through, eventually engulfing an area of 250 square miles (650sq km). Elated, the crews turned away, only to lose two Lancasters on the homeward leg.

The second wave, attacking the Sorpe, hit early trouble when two Lancasters were forced to turn back. Another was shot down by flak and a fourth crashed after hitting a power cable. Only one Lancaster, T for Tommy piloted by the American, McCarthy, reached the dam. In contrast to the other dams, which were masonry structures and had been attacked with the bouncing bombs at right angles, the Sorpe had sloping earth sides. This would force McCarthy to fly lengthways across the crest of the dam and drop his mines directly on top of it.

The approach to the Sorpe, swooping over a hillside village, was so difficult that McCarthy made 10 runs before releasing his bomb. It struck the top of the dam but, as he flew away, McCarthy realised that he had failed to breach it.

This left the reserve group, two of whose aircraft had been shot down on the outward flight. Flak damage forced a third to turn back. Of the remaining two, one attacked the Sorpe, but like McCarthy could do no more than dent the top of the dam. The other Lancaster attacked one of the secondary targets, the Ennepe, again without success. It was the last aircraft to arrive back at Scampton, at 6.15am.

Air Marshal Harris and Barnes Wallis were there for the debriefing. In all, eight of Gibson's 19 Lancasters had been lost on the operation, two of them on the return leg of the raid. Fifty-six men had failed to return, of whom only three survived as prisoners of war. The empty chairs in the squadron's mess were a heart-wrenching sight.

Guy Gibson was immediately awarded a Victoria Cross and many of his men were decorated. The Dam Busters' raid has assumed legendary status, and at the time gave an enormous psychological boost to the British morale.

It had been brilliantly conceived and heroically executed, but just how successful was it? In the Ruhr, water output had been restored within five weeks, and the Germans had offset the loss of electricity generating power by diverting supplies from elsewhere. Of some importance, however, was the destruction of farmland, bridges and machinery which diverted a considearble amount of Germany's already overstretched manpower resources to the clean-up operation.

After its epic baptism of fire, 617 Squadron went on to perform many more precision-bombing operations, including the attack which sank the battleship *Tirpitz* in November 1944. It lived on after the war and, in the 1980s, 617 became the RAF's first Tornado squadron. Ironically, perhaps, the Moehne and Sorpe dams still stand today.

BARNES WALLIS AND HIS BOUNCING BOMB

Barnes Wallis was one of Britain's greatest aero-engineers, the designer of the R100 airship and the Wellington bomber, both of which had geodetic airframes. To destroy the Ruhr dams, Wallis designed a 'bouncing bomb' which skipped over the water like a stone can be made to skim over a pond. Wallis tested the concept by catapulting marbles over water in a tin bath, firing projectiles across a lake and shooting small spheres along an indoor tank at his team's research laboratory at Weybridge.

In essence, the bomb – codenamed 'Upkeep' – was a gigantic depth charge armed with 6,600lb (3,000kg) of Torpex and designed to hit the retaining wall of the dam and then sink to about 30ft (9m) below the surface before exploding. In the winter of 1942-3 a Wellington bomber, fitted with special rotating and release gear, carried out a series of tests with the prototype on the south coast near Weymouth. However, it was not until April 1943 that the bomb was issued to the RAF, and even then it was quickly modified when it became clear that the wooden outer casing was causing it to break up when it hit the water.

After Operation Chastise, Wallis's bouncing bomb was never used again, but the brilliant engineer went on to design the massive 'Tallboy' and 'Grand Slam' bombs which were used by 617 Squadron to destroy German railway viaducts and concrete-roofed U-boat pens. After the war, Wallis pioneered swing wings for supersonic aircraft. When he died in 1977 at the age of 92, he was working on a revolutionary new airliner which would fly halfway round the world in only four hours

U-47
at Scapa Flow

At the beginning of the Second World War the submarine arm of the Kriegsmarine was a Cinderella service. Adolf Hitler was a landlubber with no grasp of the threat to Allied shipping posed by the U-boats under the command of the ambitious, incisive Captain Karl Donitz. the war was only six weeks old when one daring operation by a single U-boat was to focus the spotlight on the war-winning potential of German submarines.

Donitz had been a U-boat commander in the First World War. Now his attention was fixed on the Royal Navy's base at Scapa Flow in the Orkney Islands off the northern tip of Scotland. The warships which sheltered in Scapa Flow's vast natural harbour were strategically placed to deal with the Kriegsmarine's sorties into the North Sea and attempts to break in to the Atlantic – until the fall of France, the English Channel was a no-go area for the Kriegsmarine.

Scapa Flow also held bitter memories for Great War veterans like Donitz. It was here that the ships of the German Imperial Navy had surendered and then scuttled themselves after the defeat of Germany in 1918.

Donitz was convinced that a lone submarine could penetrate Scapa Flow's defences and launch a series of attacks which would not only alter the naval balance of power but also serve as a vital propaganda blow for the U-boat service.

Aerial reconnaissance and information gathered by the submarine *U-16* confirmed Donitz's belief that there were cracks in Scapa Flow's defences. In one of the eastern approaches to Scapa Flow, Holm Sound, German planners detected gaps in a line of sunken blockships which would enable a surfaced U-boat to break into the harbour under the cover of darkness.

The man chosen to lead this hazardous operation was one of the

BELOW: HMS *Royal Oak*, an aging leviathan launched in the First World War whose main armament of eight 15in (380mm) guns were no match for a U-boat's torpedoes.

Kriegsmarine's outstanding submarine commanders, the 31-year-old Gunther Prien, a fanatical Nazi who had been credited with the first U-boat victory of the war, on September 5 1939.

On October 8, *U-47* slipped into the North Sea from the Kiel Canal. To avoid detection, *U-47* remained submerged during the day and travelled on the surface at night. The 44-man crew slept during the daylight hours and awoke to breakfast when night fell.

U-47 reached the Orkneys on the night of the 12th. Until this point only Prien knew the object of the submarine's mission. After a night of observation, *U-47* settled on the bottom and the motors were cut. Ther crew assembled in the forward mess and were told that on the following night *U-47* would enter Scapa Flow.

Prien's last-minute preparations for the attack were meticulous. No one was to smoke in the boat or speak unnecessarily. Every man inspected his life jacket and the navigator fixed his chart. The torpedoes were armed and prepared for firing. Scuttling charges were distributed around the boat, in case *U-47* was forced to take the same desperate action as the Imperial German Navy at the end of the First World War.

At 7pm *U-47* surfaced. Prien, two officers and his bo'sun emerged on the conning tower to find the northern lights casting an alarming glow over the approaches to Scapa Flow. It seemed impossible that *U-47* could avoid being spotted, but Prien pressed on.

U-47 squeezed into Scapa Flow, scraping noisily across the cable attached to one of the blockships amd momentarily running aground. Prien ordered the instant opening of the air pressure valves and blew the flooded diving tanks, and *U-47* shook herself free.

Moments later, the U-boat was illuminated by the headlights of a civilian car on the mainland. But no one raised the alarm and Prien glided on, searching for his prey. The capital ships were no longer there, only the aging *Royal Oak*, a second-line battleship commissioned in 1916.

Prien spotted *Royal Oak* at about 1am. Behind the battleship was the seaplane tender *Pegasus*, which the U-boat commander mistook for the battleship *Repulse*.

At a range of about 300m, *U-47* fired a salvo of three torpedoes, two at the *Royal Oak* and one at *Pegasus*. Nearly four minutes elapsed before one of the torpedoes slammed into *Royal Oak*'s bow.

The battleship shivered at the impact but on board there was little alarm. It was thought to be a small internal explosion.

ABOVE: Gunther Prien in the conning tower of *U-47*, whose command he assumed just before the outbreak of war.

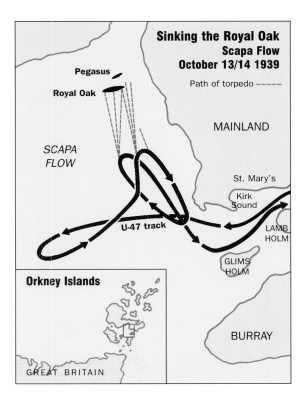

Meanwhile, Prien went about to reload his forward torpedo tubes while simultaneously firing from his rear tube.

The rear tube torpedo missed, but 12 minutes later Prien fired a second salvo which destroyed *Royal Oak*. The first torpedo hit *Royal Oak* on the starboard side under her B turret. The remaining two arrived seconds later, lifting the 32,000-ton warship out of the water.

Then *Royal Oak* settled and began to list to starboard. Chaos reigned aboard. All power had been lost and communications systems had been destroyed, Hundreds of men were trapped below by fires and jammed power-operated hatches.

Ten minutes later, *Royal Oak* turned turtle, taking with her 833 men to their deaths. As the battleship went down, *U-47* was making her escape, fighting against the current. Twisting and turning his way through a narrow but deep channel, Prien took *U-47* past the blockship and out into the North Sea. When Prien knew they were safe, he broke open a crate of beer for the crew.

U-47 reached Wilhelmshaven at 11am on the 17th, but not without surviving a depthcharging by a Royal Navy minesweeper on the 15th.

Prien and his crew were given a heroes' welcome by Admiral Donitz. The entire crew were awarded the Iron Cross 2nd Class; Prien was later decorated with the Knight's Cross by Adolf Hitler.

BELOW: *U-47* scored an early triumph in sinking the *Royal Oak*, but the Battle of the Atlantic, which lasted from the first day of the war to virtually the last, took a terrible toll on U-boat crews, claiming 26,000 killed out of 41,000 crewmen who sailed.

Donitz had been vindicated by the sinking of *Royal Oak*, and later in the war, in 1943, the U-boat arm, operating with a strength of 300 vessels, came close to winning the Battle of the Atlantic and throttling Britain's vital Atlantic supply line.

Prien did not long survive his triumph. *U-47* was sunk by the British destroyer *Wolverine* on March 8 1941 while attacking the Atlantic convoy OB293. She went down with all hands, eight of them, including Prien, veterans of the sinking of *Royal Oak*.

The Rock Force at Corregidor

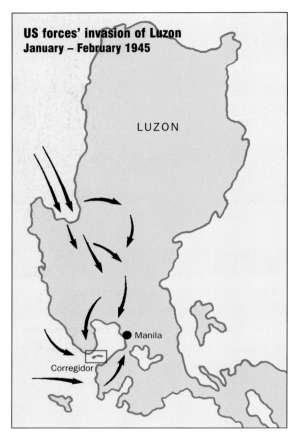

US forces' invasion of Luzon January – February 1945

LUZON

Manila

Corregidor

Corregidor

Battery Point

Rock Point

34th Infantry Regiment

North Point

Bottomside

Monkey Point

Topside

Middleside

Malinta Tunnel

SAN JOSE

Hooker Point

Golf course

503rd Para Infantry Regiment

Geary Point

US forces

Airborne assault

The capture by the Japanese of the island fortress of Corregidor, nicknamed 'The Rock', on May 6 1942 had left bitter memories of the humiliations heaped on the United States during the first six months of the war in the Pacific. An island guarding the entrance to Manila Bay, off Luzon in the Philippines, it had been heavily fortified in the aftermath of the Spanish-American War of 1898 and became known as Fort Mills.

After the American surrender of the Bataan Peninsula on April 9 1942, Fort Mills had been besieged by the Japanese, suffering a crushing aerial and artillery bombardment for almost a month. Most of Fort Mills' above-ground structures had been destroyed and its batteries put out of action.

On May 5 a force of some 2,000 Japanese infantry landed on the island, and the commander of Fort Mills, General Wainwright, surrendered the following day. In February 1942, General Douglas MacArthur, then the US commander in the Far East, had been ordered out of Luzon, leaving with the words, 'I shall return.' But it was not until the autumn of 1944 that MacArthur, now C-in-C Allied Forces Southwest Pacific, was able to persuade the American Joint Chiefs of Staff that the reconquest of the Philippines was an essential step on the way to the defeat of Japan. On October 20 1944, MacArthur did return, landing on Leyte Island. Japanese resistance on Luzon was over by the end of December and the US Sixth Army moved on to Luzon and Manila.

The plans to retake Manila included a daring airborne asault on Corregidor. The unit chosen for the operation was the 503rd Parachute Infantry Regiment, which had made its combat debut in New Guinea, performing the first Allied parachute jump in the Pacific theatre. The regiment had been held in reserve during the invasion of Leyte and then participated in the amphibious assault on Mindoro, an island to the northwest

The 503rd was supremely confident, although the attack on

Corregidor faced formidable difficulties. It would be harder to devise a more treachorous drop zone for airborne troops. The tadpole-shaped island was three and a half miles (5.6km) long and, at its narrowest point, only 600 yards (550m) wide. The most obvious drop zone would have been on the narrow neck of land which connected the head of the tadpole to its tail. Known as 'Bottomside', this was overlooked by a plateau known as 'Topside', from which the Japanese defenders of Corregidor could pour a hail of fire on the paratroops as they came down.

The commander of the 503rd PIR, Colonel George M. Jones, thus had no alternative but to land his three battalions, augmented by artillery and engineers, on two pocket-handkerchief-sized sites on Topside itself – a miniature golf course and a former parade ground. The 6,000 paratroops would be supported by an amphibious landing made by 1,000 soldiers of the 34th Infantry.

There was a second problem, as yet unknown to the Americans. Intelligence estimates of the enemy garrison at Corregidor were wide of the mark. The Americans expected to deal with about 600 troops. In fact, Corregidor was held by 6,000 battle-hardened men, including units from the Imperial Navy's special landing forces. Like the Americans, the Japanese were also labouring under a misapprehension. They had discounted the possibility of an airborne assault and expected to deal with an attack from the sea.

The operation began on February 16 after a massive preliminary bombardment which forced the defenders of Corregidor into underground bunkers and destroyed their communications system. The commander of the Japanese garrison, Captain Agira Itagaki, was now unable to conduct a co-ordinated defence of of the island.

The plan was to drop Jones's men in three waves from the few available C-47 transports at 8.30am, 12am on the 16th and 8.30am on the 17th. The C-47s would fly in low, two abreast, dropping a stick of eight men each on three separate runs over Corregidor. Timing was crucial to avoid spilling men into the sea where PT boats were positioned to deal with just such an eventuality. Lack of aircraft meant that the men would have to drop with their machine-guns and mortars strapped to their bodies. Jones calculated that he might incur up to 50 per cent casualties in the operation.

As the paratroopers floated down

ABOVE: Men of the 503rd come down in scrub-covered ground on Corregidor. Those who landed in rocky or forested areas suffered many injuries.

BELOW: A paratrooper wearing a helmet split open by sniper fire keeps careful watch for the enemy.

ABOVE: A Dakota disgorges paratroops in a dry run for the mission to recapture Corregidor.

BELOW: Paratroops move through the smouldering landscape of Corregidor. The man standing carries a small pack and water bottles on his belt. He is armed with a 0.45in Thompson sub-machine gun.

on to Corregidor there was little fire from the Japanese, who had not emerged from their bunkers and were not expecting a descent from the skies. More dangerous for the first wave were the jagged lumps of concrete scattered over the drop zones by the bombardment.

It took just under two hours for the first wave to drop on Corregidor, directed by Jones circling overhead in a C-47. An early success was scored when a group landed near Itagaki's command post, despatching him with a grenade and leaving the already isolated garison leaderless.

Jones dropped into Corregidor as the the final C-47s swept over Corregidor. By then the the paratroops had secured the whole of Topside. They had incurred 25 per cent casualties, although a high proportion of these suffered cuts and abrasions caused by hard landings.

Japanese attention was fully engaged by the airborne landings when the amphibious attack was launched by 34th Infantry Regiment on Black Beach, which lay just beneath Corregidor's tadpole head. Four waves of infantry came ashore virtually unopposed, but by the time the fifth wave arrived the defenders had regained their balance and pinned them down until the arrival of two tanks to reinforce the 75mm pack howitzers of Jones's field artillery battalion.

When his second wave had parachuted into Corregidor, Jones was able to call on 3,000 men to deal with the anticipated Japanese counter-attack. It was vital to hold Topside in order to receive air-droppped supplies and bring howitzer fire down on the enemy while the rest of Rock Force cleared the ground to the south and linked up with the infantry lodgement on Black Beach. Although he was outnumbered by about two to one, Jones had gained the upper hand, holding the high ground, deploying tanks and artillery and able to call down naval gunfire on Japanese positions.

While the Japanese launched a series of unco-ordinated attacks on the night of the 17th, Jones altered his plans. The next day his third wave came into Black Beach on landing craft, to avoid casualties, while their heavy equipment was airdropped on Topside.

After a series of suicide charges launched by the Japanese special landing forces, a major counter-attack was mounted in the early hours of the 18th. Over 500 Japanese burst from their hiding places on Topside. Nearly all of them died in bitter hand-to-hand fighting in which Private Lloyd McCarter single-handedly blunted a Japanese

charge before being mortally wounded in the chest. When he was pulled, protesting, to safety, his foxhole was surrounded by piles of enemy dead. McCarter was posthumously awarded the Congressional Medal of Honor in recognition of his courageous action.

It now remained to mop up an unknown number of Japanese who had been lurking underground in Corregidor's bunkers and tunnels since the beginning of the battle. When 2,000 of them tried to blast their way out of the Malinta tunnel, nearly all of them were killed in a series of enormous subterranean explosions. Few of the Japanese garrison were prepared to consider surrender and on the 26th the eruption of a magazine, set off by the Japanese, killed 52 Americans and wounded 144.

Within 24 hours, Corregidor had been secured. The Americans estimated the enemy death toll at 4,500, many hundreds of them blown to smithereens or buried in the warren of caves and tunnels under Fort Mills. Only 20 prisoners were taken, most of them because they had been knocked unconscious by explosions. The American casualties were 225 killed and missing and 645 wounded or injured during the landings.

To mark its role in the retaking of Corregidor, the 503rd Parachute Infantry Regiment's shoulder patch was redesigned to incorporate the 'Rock'. In the aftermath of the battle, General MacArthur visited the Rock and observed in his characteristically grandiloquent fashion, 'I see that the old flagpole still stands. Have the troops hoist the colors to its peak and let no enemy ever haul them down.'

ABOVE: An aerial view of the assault on Corregidor. The white dots in the centre of the picture are parachutes.

TOP: After the battle. The 12in guns installed on Corregidor before the outbreak of war remain today as a reminder of the men who died in the defence and recapture of the island fortress.

The French at Bir Hacheim

Above: Men of the French Foreign Legion, in distinctive kepis, move on to the attack in the Western Desert.

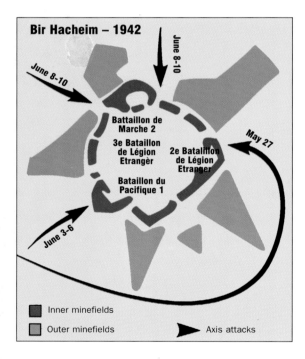

Bir Hacheim – 1942

June 8-10
June 8-10
June 8-10

Battaillon de Marche 2

3e Bataillon de Légion Etrangèr

2e Bataillon de Légion Etranger

Bataillon du Pacifique 1

May 27

June 3-6

Inner minefields
Outer minefields
Axis attacks

In the summer of 1940 the French army and nation had suffered a humiliating defeat at the hands of Germany. Two years later, at a critical point in the war in North Africa, the First Free French Brigade was desperate to redeem the honour of France in action against Rommels' Afrika Korps.

It was the Brigade's task to garrison the the ruined fort at Bir Hacheim, the most southerly point in the the British Eighth Army's defensive line in the Western Desert built to deny Rommel the port of Tobruk. The so-called Gazala Line consisted of a series of dense minefields linking a number of fortified 'boxes' designed to hold out against even the heaviest enemy attacks for several days.

If Rommel decided to launch a southern, outflanking manoeuvre, Bir Hacheim would become vital to the defence of Tobruk, menacing the Axis supply lines. Rommel's offensive began on May 26, achieving tactical surprise and in the south overrunning the 3rd Indian Motor Brigade's box five miles (8km) southeast of Bir Hacheim.

It is an irony, perhaps, that the majority of the 3,700 defenders of Bir Hacheim were not truly French. They included an infantry battalion from French Equatorial Africa, a battalion from Tahiti and a Marine battalion from Syria.

The core of the force at Bir Hacheim comprised two battalions of the Foreign Legion, the 2nd and 3rd Battalions of the 13th Demi-Brigade de la Legion Etrangere, commanded by a emigré Russian prince, Lieutenant-Colonel Amilakvari, a Georgian who had fled the Revolution and joined the Legion in 1924. Many of the legionnaires were German.

In overall command at Bir Hacheim was General Marie-Pierre Koenig, a veteran of World War I who had seen action with the Legion in Norway in 1940. Under Koenig's vigorous leadership, a network of deep shelters and trenches had been dug at Bir Hacheim, capable of housing his entire garrison. Minefields surrounded Koenig's 12-mile (20km) perimeter, forcing attackers into corridors covered by strongpoints.

On the afternoon of May 26, one of Koenig's forward patrols detected the approach of a large enemy force. That night the chilly desert air echoed to the rattling of the armour of the Italian 102nd Ariete and 101st Armoured Divisions as they manoeuvred to attack.

The Italians' 220 light and 50 medium tanks, crawling like ants across the desert, were thrown into the attack early on the morning of the 27th. Unsupported by infantry, they charged headlong through the corridors in the minefields and straight on to the 54 75mm anti-tank guns in the French strongpoints.

One of the defenders recalled: 'We held our fire and then let blaze when the enemy was only 400 yards (365km) away and continued firing until the last tank became stationary only a few yards from the muzzles of our anti-tank guns. Dashing forward, the legionnaires captured the Italian soldiers who had abandoned their burning vehicles. Some of the poor wretches were screaming with anguish and rolling on the ground to exstinguish the flames which had caught their clothes and were burning them alive.'

In spite of the carnage, a few Italian tanks broke through the French defences, only to be disposed of by legionnaires clambering on to their hulls and firing into the sight slits at point blank range. By the end of the day the Italians had withdrawn, leaving behind the gutted hulks of 32 tanks.

While heavy fighting raged to the northeast, the defenders of Bir Hacheim enjoyed a four-day lull. Eighth Army seemed to be gaining the upper hand and Koenig was ordered to send a motorised column westward across the desert to seize the Italian-held position at Ronda Segnali.

Rommel, however, beat Koenig to the punch. As the battle for the Gazala Line swung to and fro, the attention of the commander of the Afrika Korps was increasingly drawn to Bir Hacheim. Rommel decided to remove this irritating thorn in his side with a crushing air and artillery bombardment.

The German 90th Light Division and the Italian Trieste

BELOW: Legionnaires prepare for a patrol. Note their varying headgear and uniforms.

BOTTOM: The garrison of Bir Hacheim used their 75mm anti-tank guns in a mobile role, mounting them on trucks and moving them rapidly from crisis point to crisis point.

ABOVE: A motorcyclist of 21st Panzer Division churns through the desert, his sidecar armed with a machine-gun.

Division were ordered south to close the ring around Bir Hacheim, while the sky over the fortress became black with Ju 87 dive-bombers. Koenig retrieved his motorised column and the French sat out pulverising waves of Stuka attacks in their underground shelters.

On the morning of June 2 two Italian officers drove up to Bir Hacheim under a white flag, calling on Koenig to surrender. Koenig refused, as he did the next day when Rommel himself intervened. The unequal artillery duel between the French and their besiegers was resumed.

In the air, however, the Axis was not having things all its own way. On June 3 the Stukas were jumped by Hawker Hurricanes of the Desert Air Force and were driven off. In addition, vital supplies of water and ammunition were still reaching Bir Hacheim under the cover of darkness.

On June 6, after a heavy preparatory bombardment, an infantry attack was launched against Koenig's southernmost strongpoint. Advancing over open ground the attackers were mown down by machine gun fire. A second assault suffered the same fate.

Nevertheless, Bir Hacheim's days were clearly numbered. In the small hours of June 8, the last convoy slipped through the siege lines. Each man was now allowed only 2½ pints (1½ litres) of water a day. The psychological strain of continuous bombardment was beginning to take its toll.

The arrival of the last convoy coincided with a fresh series of infantry attacks, this time supported by heavy tanks. Bir Hacheim's defences were buckling; an observation post was overrun and hand-to-hand fighting broke out around several strongpoints along the northern perimeter. Koenig counterattacked with Bren gun carriers.

On the night of June 9/10, Koenig decided that the only hope lay in a breakout. But another day of savage fighting lay ahead in which tanks once again tried to bulldoze their way into Bir Hacheim while Hurricanes swept low over the battlefield strafing enemy infantry.

As night fell, Koenig's men prepared to break out to the west.

Sappers worked with feverish haste to clear a path through the minefields they had so recently laid. Trucks were dug out of their emplacements and moved into position, the noise of their motors drowned by the fire of Bir Hacheim's 75mm guns.

The legionnaires of 13th Demi-Brigade led the breakout, with the trucks following them in single file along the narrow corridor cleared by the sappers. Enemy flares lit up the night sky, illuminating the French in their eerie glow. Machine guns opened up and chaos overwhelmed the column. The trucks were caught in a nightmarish traffic jam, sitting targets for the enemy's guns. Those that attempted to crash out of the corridor were blown up by mines. Fighting spilled into the surrounding desert as small groups of Koenig's men rushed machine gun posts with fixed bayonets.

Below: Ju 87 dive-bombers in desert camouflage. By this stage in the war the Stuka had lost much of its menace and its vulnerability to fighter attack had been exposed.

Koenig knew that when dawn came up confusion would be replaced by cold-blooded massacre. In a last desperate charge his Bren gun carriers punched a hole in the enemy lines through which his remaining vehicles careered into the open desert. Koenig's car, with his female driver Susan Travers at the wheel, was riddled with bullets when they blundered into an enemy bivouac, but driver and passenger survived.

Six miles (9.5km) to the west of Bir Hacheim, the French linked up with elements of Eighth Army. Some 2,500 men had reached safety and had reawakened the fighting spirit of France.

ABOVE: A legionnaire is decorated. The defenders of Bir Hacheim had restored the fighting honour of France.

The Bridge at Remagen

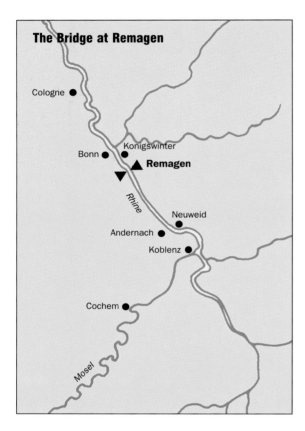

The Bridge at Remagen

By the beginning of March 1945 the Western Allies, advancing on a broad front, were closing up to the River Rhine, the last great natural barrier between them and the heart of Germany.

On March 7 the VII Corps of the US First Army had reached the Rhine at Cologne. But the Germans had destroyed all the bridges across the river. Forty-five miles (72km) to the south lay the town of Remagen, where beetling bluffs overlooked the Ludendorff railway bridge spanning the Rhine.

At 12.56pm on March 7 the men of A Company, 27th Armored Infantry Battalion, reached the top of a gorge on the west bank of the Rhine to find themselves gazing in astonishment at an intact bridge over the river.

Commanded by 22-year-old Lieutenant Karl Timmermann, A Company, travelling in half-tracks supported by four Pershing M-26 tanks, was acting as 'point' for Task Force Engeman, an all-

RIGHT: Engineers of US 1st Army struggle to rescue a comrade after the collapse of the Ludendorff bridge on March 17 1945.

FAR RIGHT: The bridge photographed only four hours before it collapsed into the Rhine.

arms formation which was part of Brigadier-General William Hogue's Combat Command B of 9th Armored Division.

The Task Force's orders were to capture Remagen before turning south to link up with other elements of 9th Armored on the River Ahr, which flows west from the Eifel Mountains. No one expected the bridge to be standing and no orders had been issued about its capture.

Timmermann and his men watched as German troops and vehicles, many of the latter horse-drawn, streamed over the bridge in a disorganised mass which even included a herd of cows being driven to the rear.

Lieutenant-Colonel Leonard Engeman was quickly on the scene. After making a swift reconnaissance he decided that he dare not risk his armour in a drive down the narrow, steep-sided road running below his vantage point into the town. It was a potential death trap.

Instead, Timmermann's company was ordered to move down a wooded track to clear the outskirts of the Remagen, after which the four Pershings, under the command of Lieutenant John Grimball, would join them. Timmermann's three platoons were soon skirmishing through the streets of Remagen, dodging from doorway to doorway, dispersing a German patrol and capturing the town's rail station.

At 2.20pm they were joined by Grimballs' tanks, which moved down to the towpath by the river and began to lay down a suppressive fire across the bridge to prevent any sudden enemy movement. German troops could be glimpsed on the east bank, sheltering in the tunnel into which the rail line ran at the base of the basalt cliff.

By 3pm, Timmermann and his No.3 Platoon, led by Sergeant Joseph Delisio, had arrived at the town's cemetery, close to the two granite topwers at the western end of the Ludendorff Bridge.

So far the Americans had encountered little resistance. The defence of Remagen had not been one of the priorities of Field Marshal Walther Model, the commander of the German Army Group B. He was looking to the north and south of Remagen for American assault crossings of the Rhine.

Thus, on March 7 the bridge at Remagen was defended by a rag-tag force consisting of a squad of engineers, 60 members of the Volkssturm (the German equivalent of the British Home Guard) and some Luftwaffe anti-aircraft gunners manning a battery of 20mm flak guns which had now begun firing at the Americans.

The local German commander, Major Willi Bratge, had been authorised to prepare the bridge for demolition, but his bridge-master, a local man, could scrape together only about 1,300lb (590kg) of low-grade industrial explosive. This had been strapped to the girders of the bridge's central span.

ABOVE: After the capture of the bridge at Remagen, the Germans subjected it to furious air and artillery attack. Frogmen also tried to bring it down. Even a V-2 rocket was fired against it, the only time this weapon was used in a tactical role.

ABOVE: A dramatic depiction of the race to seize the bridge at Remagen.

BELOW: When the bridge collapsed it pitched many engineers into the Rhine. One of the survivors is brought to safety.

The commander of the engineer squad. Captain Karl Friesenhahn, had also used some of the explosive to mine the earth approach ramp to the bridge on the west bank, which he had built to enable vehicles to drive up on the bridge and cross on wooden planks laid over the rails.

Accompanying Bratge on that fateful day was Hans Scheller, the representative of Major-General Hitzfeld, the senior officer responsible for the bridge at Remagen. Hitzfeld had ordered Scheller to keep the bridge open as long as possible as an escape route for his command, LXVII Corps.

Now, while Scheller agonised about blowing the bridge, the American tanks began nosing down the towpath. Twenty minutes later, Engeman grasped the nettle and issued a precise command to seize the Ludendorff Bridge.

Timmerman and his men now faced the daunting prospect of taking an objective which at any moment might explode beneath their feet. Within two minutes their nervous deliberations were interrupted by a heavy explosion as Friesenhahn detonated the charges on the approach ramp. When the smoke lifted – and it became clear the the bridge was still standing – Timmermann ordered his company to cross the bridge.

As the men of No.1 Platoon, led by Sergeant Mike Chinchar, scrambled over the rubble-strewn crater, there was a second explosion. The bridge rose in the air and then settled again. Scheller had finally ordered the main charges to be blown, but part of the electrical firing mechanism had failed.

Under heavy fire from the tanks on the west bank and Task Force Engeman's assault guns and mortars positioned above Remagen, one of Friesenhahn's engineers, Sergeant Faust, ran out to ignite the fuse in the manual firing box on the bridge with a flare pistol.

Faust had just regained the safety of the tunnel when the charges went off, sending huge chunks of debris crashing into the Rhine but succeeding only in twisting the central span and punching a gaping hole in the flooring.

With machine-gun fire from the bridge's eastern towers and from a sunken barge to their right flying around their ears, Timmermann's men began to zig-zag their way across the bridge.

The machine-guns in the tower were silenced and the honour of being the first Allied soldier to set foot on the east bank of the Rhine south of Holland fell to Sergeant Alex Drabika, squad leader in No.3 Platoon.

By 4pm some 75 American troops had passed safely across the bridge and were taking their first prisoners. Behind them engineers were frantically cutting cables and hurling undetonated charges into the Rhine.

As the bridgehead at Remagen expanded, the Germans threw in a series of desperate counter-attacks. For nine days the Luftwaffe tried to destroy the Ludendorff bridge and the three tactical bridges which US engineers had thrown alongside it. Finally, on March 17, the fatally weakened bridge toppled into the Rhine, killing 28 servicemen.

The German defenders of the bridge, Bratge and Friesenhahn, were tried in absentia. Friesenhahn was acquitted but Bratge was sentenced to death. It mattered little as both men were now prisoners of the Americans, whose crossing of the Rhine at Remagen had struck a powerful psychological blow at German military and civilian morale.

BELOW: Time out from war. Infantrymen of US First Army contemplate the next move in the drive into the heart of the Reich. They are armed with the Garand rifle, the US Army's standard service rifle, which was introduced in 1936.

PT-boats in the Pacific

ABOVE: *PT-463* at speed but with no torpedo tubes. When on patrol, the PT-boats usually cruised on one engine to minimise noise and wake.

BELOW: A PT-boat crew harmonise their machine guns in the summer of 1944. The gun in the foreground is a 0.50in Browning.

From the introduction of the torpedo in the 1860s, the torpedo boat has played an active role in naval warfare. In the 1930s the US Navy developed its own Patrol Torpedo (PT) Boats, principally because of a renewed interest in fast attack craft in European navies.

Displacing 34 to 38 tons, the PT-boats were powered by three-shaft petrol engines producing 4,050hp and had a maximum speed of 40 knots. They were armed with four 18- or 21in torpedo tubes, plus one 40mm and/or two 20mm guns. They also carried 0.50 heavy machine guns. Their crew numbered between 12 and 17 depending upon type.

At the beginning of the Pacific war, the PT-boats stationed in the Philippines came into the limelight thanks to the exploits of Lieutenant-Commander John Bulkeley. On the night of January 18/19 1942, a month after the Japanese invasion of the Philippines, Bulkeley, in *PT-34*, nosed into Subic Bay at a speed of 8 knots and sank a Japanese transport with a single torpedo at a range of 500 yards (460m).

Bulkeley had in fact launched two torpedoes, but one stuck halfway out of its tube with the engine racing. Without surrounding water to cool it and retard the

propellers, a torpedo on a 'hot run' will disintegrate within seconds. Acting at speed and in the dark, Chief Torpedoman Martino found the small valve in the side of the torpedo and closed the compressed air line. The torpedo stopped, but by now, as *PT-34* roared out of Subic Bay, waves were washing over its nose, turning the impeller vanes which armed the warhead. The gallant Martino leaned out and jammed the vanes with a wad of paper. The torpedo eventually tumbled into the sea.

At this stage in the war, as the Japanese swept through the Pacific, the PT-boats were the only American warships in the region, operating from improvised bases with exhausted equipment which could not be replaced from stores destroyed by enemy bombing raids. The PT-boats' brave campaign came to a climax in March 1942 when Bulkeley rescued General Douglas MacArthur from the Bataan peninsula and carried him and his family through nearly 600 miles (950km) of Japanese-dominated waters to safety on Mindanao.

MacArthur had been much impressed by the PT-boats' ability to stalk enemy warships in narrow, island-strewn waters. He urged the expansion of the PT-boat programme and arranged for Bulkeley, who was later awarded the Congressional Medal of Honor, and his colleagues to be flown out of the theatre so that they could impart their knowledge to a new generation of PT-boat crews.

Late in 1942 the expanding PT-boat force in the Pacific, based on the island of Tulagi, was involved in the naval fighting caused by Japanese attempts to reinforce their troops on nearby Guadalcanal using heavily escorted convoys known as the 'Tokyo Express'.

In common with the US Marines fighting on Guadalcanal, the PT-boat crews had to endure harsh conditions. At their primitive bases, the PT-boats had to be refuelled by hand, straining the 10-octane petrol through chamois leathers to remove the water. By day the boats were concealed under mangrove trees where they quickly became infested with rats and all manner of insect life. The men slept on board their craft, and bedding and clothes rotted in the sweltering tropical heat.

In spite of the glamour attached to the PT-boats, hurtling through the sea trailing a spectacular but tell-tale phosphorescent wake, many of their duties were mundane – carrying mail and supplies to the men on Guadalcanal and transferring men and equipment between bigger ships.

In the Battle of the Bismarck Sea at the beginning of March

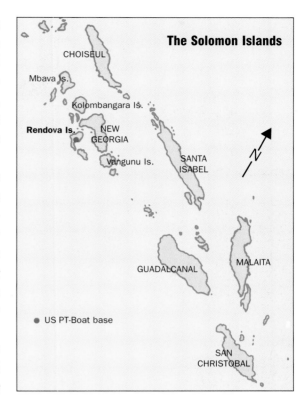

ABOVE: Reconstruction of the sinking of a Japanese freighter by *PT-38* in January 1942.

ABOVE: PT-boats race past the carrier *Hornet* at Pearl Harbor in the spring of 1942.

TOP RIGHT: John F. Kennedy is awarded the Navy and Marine Service Medal in June 1944 after his return from the Pacific.

1943, PT-boats based in New Guinea sank a large Japanese transport carrying troops from Rabaul to Lae. In the immediate aftermath of the battle it was the grim but necessary task of the PT-boats and aircraft to seek out the Japanese survivors, many of them in dinghys, machine-gunning and depth-charging them until there were none left.

That month, Lieutenant John F. Kennedy was posted to the South Pacific as a replacement to take command of *PT-109*. By August of that year the tide of Japanese conquest in the Pacific was in retreat. In the Solomons chain the principal Allied objectives were the islands of Bougainville and New Georgia.

On the night of August 1 *PT-109*'s squadron sailed from its base at Lumbari Island to patrol the Blackett Strait, which separates the island of Vila from New Georgia and through which the Japanese were running the Tokyo Express to reinforce their garrison on Vella Lavella and the airstrip at Munda on New Georgia. The squadron's task was to intercept and attack the Tokyo Express on its way in and out of the Blackett Strait.

PT-109 missed the convoy on its inward journey, taking evasive action after being caught in a destroyer's searchlight. Later that night, which was dark and starless, the PT-boat formed part of a picket line waiting to catch the Japanese on their return journey. At about 2.30am on August 2, while idling with only one of her three engines turning over, *PT-109* was rammed by the destroyer *Amagiri*. She was sliced in two and her fuel tank exploded. Kennedy gave the order to abandon ship.

Daylight found the survivors of the ramming clinging to part of their boat's hull. Two of the 13-man crew had been lost and a third, Patrick McMahon, was badly wounded. From their exposed position, Kennedy and his men could see activity on a nearby Japanese-occupied island.

That night, Kennedy and his crew paddled for five hours behind a plank salvaged from the wreckage of PT-109 to an island some three miles (5km) away. Kennedy swam breaststroke, pulling the wounded man behind him by clenching his teeth on a strap from McMahon's Mae West.

Having reached temporary safety, Kennedy swam out into the strait with a lantern in the hope of attracting a passing PT-boat, a hazardous sortie in which he was nearly swept away. The survivors then made a second long swim to a larger island, Kennedy again towing the helpless McMahon. Here they found a cache of

Japanese food and a native canoe. When Kennedy and another shipmate, George Ross, attempted to clear the island's reef in the canoe, they were nearly swept away in a squall.

Kennedy was unaware that on the morning after the sinking of *PT-109*, what was left of its capsized hull had been spotted by an Australian 'Coastwatcher', Lieutenant A.R. Evans, from his secret outpost on the volcanic outcrop of Kolombangara. Coastwatchers were an organisation of courageous intelligence-gathering operators working mainly from hidden bases behind enemy lines and reporting by radio on Japanese troop, ship and aircraft movements. Two natives employed by the Coastwatchers joined Kennedy's party, and they helped in his search for a boat which could be used to take him and his crew to safety. The search was unsuccessful, so Kennedy gave the natives a message encased in a coconut shell to take back to their Coastwatcher commander.

But it was Evans' sighting and the despatch of a search party to find the survivors, rather than the message Kennedy had scrawled and placed in a coconut, that led to the rescue. On August 7 seven

natives in a war canoe arrived to take Kennedy to Evans. The rest is history. Jack Kennedy became a war hero when journalists seized hold of the story and in 1960 became President of the United States. Coastwatcher Evans attended Kennedy's inauguration parade, which was also graced by a mock-up of *PT-109*—and the famous coconut, encased in plastic, took pride of place on the desk in the Oval Office.

ABOVE: Lieutenant John F. Kennedy (far right) and members of the crew of *PT-109*, a warship which would loom large in the Kennedy legend from his earliest days as a politician to his occupation of the White House.

US Rangers at Pointe du Hoc

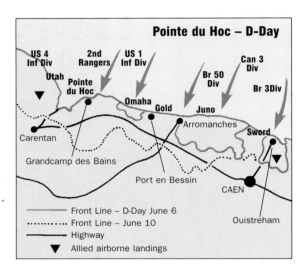

Pointe du Hoc – D-Day

US 4 Inf Div — Utah
2nd Rangers — Pointe du Hoc
US 1 Inf Div — Omaha — Gold
Br 50 Div
Can 3 Div
Br 3Div
Juno — Arromanches
Sword
Carentan
Grandcamp des Bains
Port en Bessin
CAEN
Ouistreham

— Front Line – D-Day June 6
...... Front Line – June 10
— Highway
▼ Allied airborne landings

On D-Day, June 6 1944, the US 2nd Ranger Battalion was assigned one of the toughest targets of all. The Rangers had been ordered to silence the menacing battery of six 155mm guns sited on the sheer cliffs at Pointe du Hoc, a razor-like promontory which jutted out into the sea 5 miles (8km) west of US V Corps' landing area on Omaha Beach. These guns were a menace to the Allied invasion forces. Their range stretched from the eastern edge of Omaha Beach to north of US VII Corps's Utah Beach. Their fire could also be trained on the invasion fleet lying offshore.

Bombers of the US 9th Air Force would have a preliminary crack at the battery, but if a combination of aerial bombardment and naval gunfire failed to penetrate its concrete casemates, it would be the Rangers' unenviable task, two hours before the landings went in, to finish the job by scaling the 100ft (30m) cliffs and wiping out the German garrison.

In command of the operation was a hard-driving Texan, Lieutenant-Colonel James Rudder. Considering the problems which faced him, Rudder turned to the London Fire Brigade, who devised a 100ft (30m) turntable ladder mounted on the bed of a two-and-a-half ton amphibious truck (DUKW) which would send his Rangers shooting to the top of the cliffs. Two DUKWs carried the machine-gun-enhanced ladders. Two more were to carry the support weapons which the assault teams would need to hold the the clifftop until the Rangers were relieved by infantry from Omaha Beach.

The position at Pointe du Hoc was a formidable target, and there were many who considered it virtually impregnable. Rudder was informed by one Navy officer that 'two old ladies with brooms' would be able to sweep his three companies of Rangers off the shingle beach below. But Rudder, an exceptionally tough

BELOW: The Stars and Stripes flies over the beach at Pointe du Hoc as Rangers escort their German prisoners into captivity.

commander, who had overseen his Rangers' training on the cliffs at Bude, in the English West Country, was confident that they were up to the task.

On D-Day, Rudder ran into trouble from the moment he set sail at 0430hrs. Heavy seas swamped two of his supply craft, which were lost with vital supplies of ammunition and rations. As they approached the French coast, Rudder watched from the bridge of the landing ship *Ben My Chree* as the battleship USS *Texas* hurled 14in (355mm) shells in the direction of Pointe du Hoc. Then, at 6am, 14 USAAF medium bombers flew overhead to pound the battery. At 6.30am Rudder's binoculars were still sweeping the horizon for the knife-edge promontory of Ponte du Hoc. His British naval escort had taken Rudder's task force 2 miles (3.2km) east of the target, lining up on another promontory, Point de la Percee. The task force had to go about and fight its way back to its objective, running parallel to the cliffs and attracting enemy fire all the way.

Waiting for the Rangers at Pointe du Hoc were 125 German troops from the experienced Infantry Regiment 726 and 85 gunners of the 2nd Battery of Coastal Artillery's Regiment 1260. The Rangers arrived over an hour after the naval bombardment of Pointe du Hoc had lifted. As their landing craft rasped ashore on the beach beneath the cliffs, the German troops appeared above them, like medieval warriors on the battlements of a castle.

While two destroyers raked the clifftop with fire, the Rangers rushed to the base of the cliff. A series of loud reports signalled the firing of grappling hooks to the top of the cliff but many rose for only 30 feet (9m) before clattering back on to the beach, their lines sodden by seawater. Others, fired with extra rockets, took hold. Nevertheless, the slippery clay which coated the cliffs made them all but impossible to climb. Men slithered down into gulleys, dislodging those struggling up behind them. Rudder himself was sent bowling down the lower slopes of the cliff by a chunk of chalk broken off by the naval gunfire. The Germans slung an 8in (200mm) shell over the edge of the cliff; its detonation sent more men flying.

On the heavily cratered beach the DUKWs launched from their LCTs (Landing Craft Tank) lying 400 yards (365m) offshore were inching their way towards the base of the cliff but were still not close enough to extend their ladders. Then the naval bombardment came to the Rangers' aid. Shelling from the warships had collapsed a section of cliff into a huge mound on top of which an extension ladder with a toggle rope attachment was erected. As the Rangers fought their way up the cliff the German defenders began to cut the ropes. The topmost Rangers sheltered in niches below the edge of the cliff while the bodies of dead and wounded comrades plunged past them. Finally the DUKWs' extension ladders went up. The men at the top of the ladders clung precariously to them as they rose over the cliff edge, pouring fire from the Lewis guns into the German emplacements.

BACKGROUND PIC: The razor-sharp promontory at Pointe du Hoc, a target thought by many to be impregnable. This was not a view shared by the commander of the Rangers.

BELOW: General Lucien Truscott, who played an important role in the formation of the Rangers. He commanded VI Corps in Italy in 1944 and later in the South of France. At the end of the war, Truscott assumed command of US Fifth Army in Italy.

ABOVE: The way to the top. After the battle Rangers demonstrate how they climbed the cliffs.

Within half an hour of landing, over 100 Rangers had gained a foothold on the cliff edge. Below them the beach was dotted with the bodies of their comrades and many others, dead or mortally wounded, were stuck fast in the clay of the cliff face. In front of them lay a lunar landscape carved out by the preliminary bombardment. Lieutenant-Colonel Rudder, established in a command post in a niche at the cliff edge, flashed a signal to Texas, 'Praise be!', the code for 'All men up the cliff'.

The Rangers fanned out through the battery, winkling the Germans out in a series of bitterly contested section attacks. The battery's reinforced concrete observation post, undamaged by air and naval bombardment, was put out of action with a bazooka. Behind them they left empty casemates and gun emplacements. But Allied bombing in the build-up to D-Day meant that the 155mm guns had never been installed but kept inland. The empty positions had been reported to London by the French Resistance, but the information had been ignored.

Already Rudder's three companies were organising defensive positions no more than 100 yards (30m) inland and were sending out patrols. One of these patrols, moving down the road which runs parallel to the cliffs, stumbled on five guns in an open emplacement from which they could have hit the invasion beaches. They were quickly put out of action. Another patrol found the 155mm

guns, brand new, greased and still in their packing cases. The Rangers ensured that they never fired a shot in anger.

By now one-third of Rudder's men had been killed and he was running out of ammunition. The Rangers were coming under fire from an 88mm anti-aircraft battery to the west which the Rangers attacked but failed to put out of action. While Rudder radioed for reinforcements, the German 726th Regiment was probing the Rangers' perimeter, held at bay by naval gunfire. Relief was slow in coming from Omaha Beach, where V Corps had suffered heavy casualties. Gradually, Rudder's perimeter shrank into the shell-churned terrain around his headquarters.

In the late afternoon of the 7th, the Rangers attempted to break out to join hands with 5th Rangers, who were fighting their way to Pointe du Hoc from Vierville, on the western edge of Omaha Beach. The Germans anticipated the move and beat Rudder's men back. It was not until the morning of the June 8 that 5th Rangers arrived and brought the ordeal of Rudder's men to an end. The relief column was greeted by an unforgettable sight, a cratered landscape littered with the wreckage of war. From their defensive positions Rudder's exhausted Rangers rose to greet their brothers-in-arms. Only 50 men of the original force of 200 had survived the fight for Pointe du Hoc.

ABOVE: Rangers hone their skills in unarmed combat in Britain's West country in the run-up to D-Day. Rudder's training regime was as tough as any in the US Army.

LEFT: The success of the landings in Normandy owed much to the courage of small units like the Rangers, tasked with seizing and holding tough objectives.

The Nelson Touch

ABOVE: Captain Robert Sherbrooke, commander of the destroyer *Onslow* and hero of the Battle of the Barents Sea.

RIGHT: The cruiser *Sheffield* at Murmansk with the minesweeper *Seagull*. *Sheffield* was tasked with the protection of convoy JW51B in the last stages of its journey.

BELOW: *Onslow* butts through a choppy sea in the company of HMS *Ashanti*.

After Hitler's invasion of the Soviet Union in June 1941, Britain, followed by the United States after its entry into the war, strove to keep the Russians supplied with weapons and raw materials. This meant despatching convoys around North Cape to the ports of Archangel and Murmansk through some of the most hostile seas in the world.

In winter, polar pack ice crept south, forcing the convoys to pass close to the Luftwaffe's northernmost bases. The retreat of the ice in the summer enabled the convoys to take a more northerly route, although in the perpetual daylight they remained vulnerable to attack by aircraft and the Kriegsmarine's surface ships and U-boats.

The seamen on the Arctic convoys were exposed to perpetual danger from weather and enemy warships. In sub-zero temperatures, exposed metal fittings could rip the skin off a man's bare hand; any man overboard was assumed lost, dead, within minutes of immersion in the icy waters of the Arctic. In July 1942 two-thirds of Convoy PQ-17 had been destroyed when its covering force had been mistakenly removed by the Admiralty and the convoy itself ordered to scatter. The lost cargoes included 210 aircraft, 430 tanks and 3,350 motor vehicles.

After the PQ17 disaster, there was a lull in the Arctic convoys

while great masses of Allied shipping were assembled for the Torch landings in North Africa. Convoy activity was resumed in December 1942, and the last day of the year found the British destroyer *Onslow*, commanded by Captain Robert Sherbrooke, leading the escort screen of Convoy JW51B bound for Murmansk. Convoy JW51A had preceded them, arriving in Murmansk on December 25. JW51A's cruiser escorts, *Sheffield* and *Jamaica*, under the command of Rear Admiral Robert Burnett, had turned around and were steaming south to support JW51B.

Built at Clydebank in 1941, *Onslow* was a 'Q' class destroyer with a complement of 217 men. Her armament comprised four 4.7in guns, one 4in AA gun, four 2-pounder guns and eight torpedo tubes. She was supported by five destroyers, two corvettes, a minesweeper and two armed trawlers.

That day the Kriegsmarine was also on the move. Early in the evening of December 30 a German squadron consisting of the pocket battleship *Lutzow*, the cruiser *Admiral Hipper*

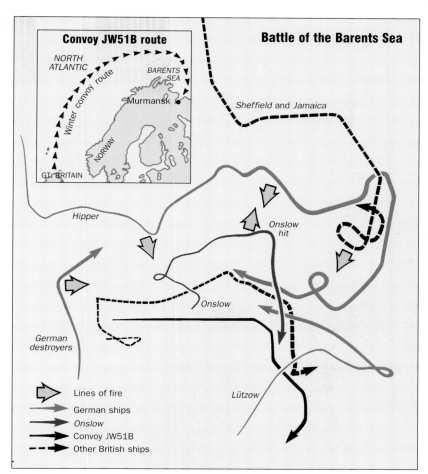

Battle of the Barents Sea

Convoy JW51B route

Lines of fire
German ships
Onslow
Convoy JW51B
Other British ships

and six destroyers, under the command of Vice-Admiral Oscar Kummetz, left Altenfjord in northern Norway to intercept JW51B.

Kummetz planned to launch converging attacks on the convoy with *Admiral Hipper* and three destroyers from the north and *Lutzow* and three destroyers from the south.

Kummetz's force closed with the convoy, and at 8.30am on December 31 the destroyer *Obdurate* signalled Sherbrooke that two of *Hipper*'s destroyers had been sighted. Just over an hour later, in poor visibility, *Onslow*'s lookouts made out the chilling profile of *Admiral Hipper*. Sherbrooke immediately signalled Admiral Burnett that a heavy enemy unit was about to attack the convoy.

The destroyers *Onslow* and *Orwell* immediately engaged *Hipper*, although they were outranged by the cruiser's 8in guns. A game of cat and mouse ensued, as the destroyers made smoke and slipped in and out of concealing snow showers to harass *Hipper*. At 10.20am *Onslow*'s luck ran out when she was hit by three 8in shells.

The results were devastating. *Onslow*'s A and B 4.7in guns were knocked out and most of their crews killed. One of the shells hit the funnel, sending a shower of splinters on to the crowded bridge. One of the splinters caught Captain Sherbrooke full in the face, knocking his left eye out of its socket and leaving it hanging down his cheek. Sherbrooke remained conscious and refused to leave the bridge, despatching damage and fire control parties throughout his ship.

The *Onslow* was in a sorry state with 40 dead and wounded, both forward guns destroyed, severe damage to the engines and a bad list to starboard. As the damage control parties fought to keep the stricken destroyer alive, she withdrew from the action while her three sister ships attempted to distract *Hipper*.

Only when command of the flotilla had been handed over to Lieutenant David Kinloch of HMS *Obedient* did Sherbrooke go below to receive treatment for his wounds.

Pausing only to destroy the minesweeper *Bramble*, which was searching for convoy stragglers, Kummetz pressed on to deal with JW51B. The battered *Onslow* took up station ahead of the convoy with the destroyer *Achates*, while the others stayed astern.

At about 11am *Hipper* came into action again. A hail of shells slammed in to *Achates*, killing her captain and many of her crew. As *Achates* slowly zigzagged away from the action,

TOP: HMS *Onslow* is cheered into port after her famous and heroic action in the Barents Sea.

ABOVE: The view from the bridge of the heavy cruiser *Admiral Hipper* whose main armament consisted of eight 8in guns.

Obdurate and *Obedient* were also hit.

At this point *Hipper* turned away, her commander fearful of torpedo attack, only to come under fire from the approaching *Jamaica* and *Sheffield*, which opened up with their 24 6in guns at a range of 16,000 yards (14,600m). *Hipper* was hit several times before she hauled round in a circle and headed away to the southeast.

Lutzow also beat a retreat, having lost the convoy in a snow squall, found it again and opened fire. But when threatened by the destroyers, the pocket battleship turned away. In the last moments of the engagement, *Sheffield* sank the destroyer *Friedrich Eckholdt*, which in the deteriorating visibility had mistaken the British cruisers for its own force.

The convoy and its escorts were left to lick their wounds. *Achates* had to be abandoned, with the loss of 57 of her crew. *Onslow* limped on while the ship's surgeon performed amputations and dressed grievous wounds in semi-darkness. Captain Sherbrooke was in such bad shape that a shot of morphine had little effect.

Careful pumping and counter-flooding kept the destroyer afloat and able to maintain a speed of 20 knots. She arrived in Murmansk the next morning. Sherbrooke's wounds were too severe to expose them to the primitive medical facilities at Murmansk, and he was returned to England early in January, a shell splinter still in his face.

Onslow arrived at Scapa Flow on February 4, where she was laid up until the following May. Captain Sherbrooke, who had shown the Nelson touch in what became known as the Battle of the Barents Sea, was awarded the Victoria Cross.

More important, perhaps, were the strategic consequences of the destroyers' gallantry. Hitler was so enraged by the poor showing of his heavy units in the action that he replaced Admiral Erich Raeder as chief of the German navy with Admiral Donitz. The majority of the fleet's surviving heavy ships were confined to training duties in the Baltic and work on the unfinished aircraft carrier *Graf Zeppelin* was halted.

BELOW: Showing signs of battle, but unbowed, the *Onslow* returns to Scapa Flow after the Battle of the Barents Sea.

The Marines at Iwo Jima

ABOVE: One of the most famous photographs of the war – US Marines placing the Stars and Stripes atop Mount Suribachi on the island of Iwo Jima.

BELOW: Marines hug the volcanic ash on the beaches at Iwo Jima in the first phase of the assault.

By the beginning of 1945, after the capture of the Marianas and the securing of the Philippines, the war in the Pacific was moving into its final phase. Blocking the American path to the home islands of Japan were the islands of Okinawa and Iwo Jima, the latter a mere speck in the ocean only eight miles square (20sq km). But Iwo Jima, with its two airfields, and a third under construction, was just two hours flying time from Japan and a vital part of the Japanese inner defensive ring. The Japanese high command saw Iwo Jima as an unsinkable aircraft carrier from which it could launch harassing attacks against the American forces massing against Japan and also monitor the increasingly heavy bombing raids hammering Japan's war industry.

Iwo Jima was also an administrative part of Japan. Its loss would deal a mortal blow to morale. As a result, the 'gateway to Japan' defended by Lieutenant-General Todomichi Kuribyashi was heavily fortified with 800 pillboxes, three miles (5km) of tunnels and extensive minefields and trench systems manned by 22,000 men prepared to sell their lives for Japan. Todomichi had no intention of defending the beaches. He had ordered his men to hold their fire until the Americans had landed and started to move inland. He told the garrison, 'Do not go and get them. Stay in your holes and let them come and get you.' Kuribyashi expected each of his men to take at least ten Americans with him.

The US 4th and 5th Divisions of Major-General Harry Schmidt's US V Amphibious Corps were tasked with the landings, with 3rd Marine Division initially held back as a reserve. After a massive naval and air bombardment, the assault on Iwo Jima went in at 9am on February 19. Iwo Jima presented a daunting sight as the landing craft churned in. Its beaches, black with volcanic dust,

were dominated by the sugarloaf of Mount Suribachi, an extinct volcano, on the southwest tip of the island.

The 4th Marine Division was on the right flank, the 5th on the left. The landing was easy enough and within half an hour all the assault forces were ashore. They had met only desultory sniping and mortar fire.

It was not until the Marines had pushed 200 yards (180m) inland, wading through the black sand, that the defenders of Iwo Jima opened up. The grim battle for the island had begun.

Tasked with taking Mount Suribachi was 5th Division's 28th Regiment, commanded by the gangling Colonel Harry B. 'Harry the Horse' Liversedge who, ironically, had been born in Volcano, California. Liversedge's plan was to cut across the island at its 750yd (685m)-wide isthmus, then wheel to the left to take Suribachi.

It was savage fighting all the way. To the Marines inching their across the desolate scrubland which surrounded Suribachi, there seemed to be a Japanese pillbox every 10 feet (3m). The mountain itself, looming over the battlefield, seemed to take on an evil life of its own.

With so many troops squeezed into so small a space, there was much hand-to-hand fighting. As he approached a pillbox, Private First Class Leo Jez was suddenly confronted by a sword-wielding

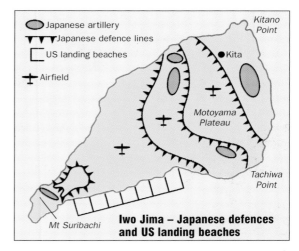

Iwo Jima – Japanese defences and US landing beaches

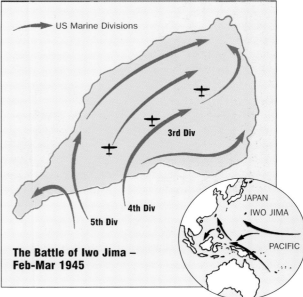

The Battle of Iwo Jima – Feb-Mar 1945

LEFT: Men of Fourth Division on the beach at Iwo Jima, with landing ships in the background. Heavy fighting erupted only when the Marines had pushed inland.

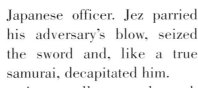

Japanese officer. Jez parried his adversary's blow, seized the sword and, like a true samurai, decapitated him.

An equally surreal touch was added by the regimental mascot, a fox terrier called George, who scampered happily through the carnage and survived the battle. His master did not, nor did the 28th's command post, which took a direct hit from a mortar.

By the night of the 25th the enemy defences at the base of Suribachi had been largely destroyed. Although the Japanese were still holed up in dozens of mountainside caves – and in prepared defensive positions on the west side of Suribachi – it was decided to send a patrol up the north face of the mountain to determine the best route to seize the high ground.

At dawn on the 23rd, a patrol of 40 American soldiers began the climb, moving rapidly to the lip of Suribachi's crater, where, at 10.37am, they planted a small flag tied to a stick. By midday the mountain was surrounded and mopping-up operations had begun.

Later that day the small flag used by the patrol in the initial raising of the colours was taken down and replaced by a larger flag attached to a taller and more sturdy pole. It was the erection of this flag, photographed by Associated Press photojournalist Joe Rosenthal, which produced one of the enduring images of the war in the Pacific.

28th Marines had been expexted to capture Suribachi in 12 hours. It had taken four four days and cost 904 casualties including 212 dead

When the larger flag went up, its was seen from the isthmus, giving a shot in the arm to the Marines locked in battle below. The raising of the flag did not mark the end of the fighting on Iwo Jima; it was merely the prelude to a struggle which was to last until March 16.

At the moment the flag appeared atop Suribachi, 5th Division was moving northward up the west coast of Iwo Jima to find its progress barred by a major defensive line, on the Montoyama plateau, behind which lay the bulk of the island's defenders in one of the most fiendish combinations of broken terrain and defensive strength encountered during the war.

The next day the 3rd Division came ashore to join the fighting in the centre of the line while 4th Division began to batter at the northeastern and eastern defences.

Most of the amtracs which would have made the

BELOW: Marines move cautiously through a wasteland of shattered tree stumps. Japanese resistance was fanatical and only 212 of the garrison surrendered after three weeks of savage fighting.

task easier had stuck on the beaches and been destroyed at close range by Japanese artillery. The wounded on the beaches also came under heavy fire while they awaited evacuation. The war correspondent Robert Sherrod, who had covered many amphibious landings from Tarawa onwards, thought that Iwo Jima was the worst battle he had ever seen, in which men died 'with the greatest possible violence'.

On the Montoyama plateau, advances were measured in tens rather than hundreds of yards. In the attack on Hill 362A, three of the men who had raised the flags on Mount Suribachi were killed. By nightfall on the 28th, however, the hill was in American hands and 'Harry the Horse' Liversedge had won his second Navy Cross.

By March 9 the men of 28th Marines could glimpse the sea on the northern coast of the island, but it was not until the 16th that Iwo Jima was declared secure. Mopping-up operations continued well into April.

In taking Iwo Jima the Americans had suffered 6,891 killed and 18,700 wounded. Of the 3,900 men of 28th Marines who had landed on February 19, only 600 remained fit for action. Just 212 of the Japanese garrison chose to surrender. Their commander had died in the front line.

Above the living and the dead the Stars and Stipes rippled and snapped in the wind. In the words of Admiral Nimitz, commander of the US Pacific Fleet, uncommon valour on Iwo Jima was a common virtue.

TOP: Mopping-up on Iwo Jima. Two Japanese soldiers surrender to a Marine. The Japanese code of *bushido* laid down that death was infinitely preferable to the dishonour of surrender, a factor which contributed to the heavy casualties suffered by the Marines in the island fighting in the Pacific.

ABOVE: Riflemen of 23rd Marines in action from a position next to a captured enemy strongpoint.

The SAS, Northwest Europe

The British Special Air Service was formed in Egypt in July 1941 by the then Captain David Stirling and was designated L Detachment of the Special Air Services Brigade, a higher formation which did not as yet exist. It was Stirling's firm belief that small units of highly trained and motivated men could, in the right circumstance, exert an influence greater than a numerically stronger force. Stirling's initial targets were German and Italian airfields in North Africa. Working in co-operation with the Long Range Desert Group, the SAS eventually destroyed over 400 enemy aircraft on the ground and quantities of fuel, ammunition and stores.

The SAS's favoured mode of transport was the heavily armed jeep, capable of travelling long distances and harassing Axis communications. Following the summer of 1942, Stirling's ever-growing private army became 1st Special Air Service Regiment (1 SAS); a 2nd SAS Regiment was raised for service with Allied 1st Army in Tunisia. The men who fought in the SAS had to be mobile, flexible, unorthodox, persistent and extremely fit.

At the beginning of 1944 the Special Air Service Brigade became a reality, comprising five regiments, of which two were

BELOW: Somewhere in occupied France, Resistance workers blow up a bridge. In the build-up to and immediate aftermath of Overlord, the SAS did much to co-ordinate Resistance activity.

French and one Belgian. The SAS also took under its wing a squadron of the field intelligence-gathering unit, the British GHQ Liaison Regiment, Royal Armoured Corps, codenamed Phantom. The SAS Brigade strength was some 2,500.

The SAS was to play an important part in Overlord, the invasion of Normandy. SAS teams were to be inserted by air, with their jeeps and equipment, into the German rear areas to co-ordinate Resistance activity, undertake acts of sabotage and disrupt German communications. Before the Allied landings on June 6 1944 several SAS reconnaissance parties were air-dropped into France to prepare the ground.

One of the first SAS operations in France, codenamed 'Houndsworth', began on D-Day itself when 18 officers and 125 men of 1 SAS cut the Dijon-Paris railway line in no fewer than 22 places. Houndsworth was not wound up until the beginning of September, by which time the regiment had killed or wounded 220 Germans and taken 132 prisoners.

Operation 'Gain', which 1 SAS launched later in June with the aim of cutting the rail links between Rambouillet and Chartres, was conducted in typical SAS style. The men drove their jeeps about quite openly, parking them beside the tracks they were about to blow up. When they observed that the Germans used their headlights, they did the same. On occasion the jeeps found themselves dodging in and out of heavily armed German convoys.

The jeeps, armed with twin Vickers .303 machine-guns at the front and rear, were formidable offensive weapons, used to shoot up transporters, trucks, petrol carriers and trains at close range. With an average rate of fire of 1,200 rounds a minute, the Vickers could reduce a truck to matchwood. The ear-shattering noise it produced was also a valuable psychological weapon. Jeeps were also equipped with a 2-inch (5cm) thick windscreen, carried smoke canisters and often towed .75in howitzers and 6 pounders. Every third jeep carried mortars. A jeep on operations, festooned with weaponry, ammunition, demolition charges and extra fuel, was a dangerous mount. Of the jeeps operating in Europe about one-third were lost, although most of their crews managed to get away.

Everywhere they went, the SAS units inflicted casualties out of all proportion to their own numbers. They usually had the advantage of surprise, vastly superior firepower and experience and local knowledge provided by members of the Resistance. When a German patrol discovered an SAS hide-out, it usually meant the end of the German patrol.

When the Germans began to withdraw from Normandy, the SAS went over to harassing their retreat. In one operation a mixed force of the Belgians from 5 SAS and men from 1 and 2 SAS were 'blind-dropped' south of Rouen in two groups. They inflicted much damage at close quarters on the enemy without once being counter-attacked themselves. At this stage in the war the Germans had too much on their minds to deal with the elusive SAS.

BACKGROUND PIC: Moonlight descent. SAS activities in northwest Europe were often hampered by two factors: the presence of the SAS in certain areas might signpost an imminent Allied move; and it might also bring down German reprisals on the local population.

BELOW: Lieutenant-Colonel R. B. 'Paddy' Mayne, a former Irish rugby international and legendary SAS man who was in at the beginning in the Western Desert with David Stirling.

ABOVE: Men of the French Resistance man a barricade in Paris shortly before its liberation by the Allies. At great personal risk, Resistance workers provided SAS units operating behind enemy lines with vital local knowledge.

In Operation 'Loyton', launched in the Vosges, the aim was to disrupt communications between Germany and France from a base established near the town of Moussey. Loyton was supposed to take ten days but lasted two months, a delay caused by a supply breakdown in American General Patton's Third Army, which was advancing on Nancy. During Loyton 28 captured SAS men were executed by the Gestapo. The Germans also took savage reprisals on the gallant people of Moussey, who had been unstinting in the aid they had given the SAS men and refused to reveal the location of the SAS base, even under cruel torture.

At the time, Moussey seemed a failure, but, as one of the men involved, Captain John Hislop, recalled: 'It was not until later that the discovery was made of the disruption and alarm to which our presence gave rise among the Germans. The troops in the area were kept in a state of permanent tension, never knowing when they were likely to be ambushed, or blown up by a mine laid in the road, or the strength of our force and how to pin it down. ... Finally an entire SS Division was withdrawn for the sole purpose of destroying us ... the comparatively little damage we inflicted was counterbalanced by the number and quality of the German troops which our presence tied down.'

In the winter of 1944 the SAS saw hard fighting alongside the partisans in Italy before joining the drive into the Reich which ended the war. An SAS unit had the honour of capturing the German foreign minister, Joachim von Ribbentrop, while in Norway. The task of disarming the 300,000-strong army of occupation was given to 1 and 2 SAS. The Germans were not inclined to argue with them.

The SAS's final score in northwest Europe was nearly 8,000 enemy killed or badly wounded and nearly 5,000 taken prisoner. The last figure does not include an entire German division which surrendered to the SAS in France when it found its line of retreat

LEFT: SAS men photographed in June 1944 during Operation Bull Basket, one of a number of strategic operations covering areas over 50 miles (80km) ahead of the Allied advance which persuaded the Germans to divert large numbers of troops to deal with tiny units of the SAS. Some 43 similar operations were mounted in the four months after D-Day.

BELOW: An SAS man searches a civilian for weapons in November 1944. As they retreated, the Germans left behind agents posing as civilians or refugees.

blocked. The SAS also destroyed or captured some 700 motor vehicles, derailed 33 trains and destroyed 29 locomotives. They also provided the Allied armies with a stream of intelligence – on one memorable occasion coming up with the entire German order of battle in the Somme area, received from an observant French doctor and retained after a fierce battle with a German armoured unit when, for once, the SAS were taken by surprise.

The presence of the SAS raised the spirits of the Resistance and lowered that of the enemy. Of the 2,000 SAS men engaged in operations in northwest Europe, 330 were killed or seriously wounded.

The SAS was disbanded at the end of the war and then reborn in 1947 as a Territorial unit, 21 SAS. A new chapter in the story of the SAS was about to begin....

Gran Sasso Rescue

ABOVE: Hitler's favourite commando, Lieutenant-Colonel Otto Skorzeny. After rescuing Mussolini, his subsequent wartime exploits included sowing confusion behind Allied lines during the Ardennes offensive in December 1944, using English-speaking Germans wearing American uniforms. Skorzeny was later tried for war crimes and acquitted.

ABOVE RIGHT: The Albergo-Rifugia Hotel, where Mussolini was held after being overthrown.

On July 25 1943, two weeks after the Allied invasion of Sicily, the Italian dictator Benito Mussolini was arrested and a new government, headed by Marshal Badoglio, opened secret negotiations with the Allies.

Mussolini was eventually moved in great secrecy to an island off the coast of Sardinia and then to a remote hotel in the Gran Sasso mountains. Meanwhile, at Rastenburg, his headquarters in the dank pine forests of East Prussia, Adolf Hitler had decided to rescue his old fascist comrade in a daring commando raid.

The man he chose for the task was the tall, heavily scarred 35-year-old Captain Otto Skorzeny, a Nazi Party veteran who had fought with the Waffen-SS in France, Yugoslavia and Russia. In 1943 he had transferred to the Fuhrer's Security Office, assigned to undercover work.

Skorzeny was summoned to Rastenburg and given the assignment pesonally by the Fuhrer. Hitler impressed on Skorzeny the secrecy of the mission, adding that he would be under the nominal

command of General Kurt Student, commander of Germany's airborne forces.

Skorzeny requested 50 men for the mission and subnmitted a list of requirements ranging from machine guns to priests' robes. Then, accompanied by Student, he flew to Rome.

It took several weeks of investigation, including a trip to Sardinia, to pick up Il Duce's trail. Intelligence suggested that Mussolini was being held at the Albergo-Rifugia, a hotel 6,500ft (1,980m) above a valley near Lake Bracciano in the mountains north of Rome. The location had been turned into a military camp, the only access to which was by cable car.

Skorzeny despatched several of his men to reconnoiter the area but they coud not penetrate the dense cordon of Italian troops thrown around Mussolini's prison. On September 8, Skorzeny himself undertook a hazardous aerial reconnaissance, hanging half-freezing from an He 111 bomber with a camera as it circled the Gran Sasso.

The Rescue of Il Duce

Lake
Bracciano

Bracciano ●

● ROME

ROME ●

ITALY

Above: A haggard Mussolini is squeezed into the Fieseler Storch, along with Skorzeny and the pilot, who faced the difficult task of flying the overloaded light plane off the mountain.

Skorzeny's suspicions were confirmed by rumours that everyone in the hotel had been evicted to make way for Mussolini.

The hotel was situated atop a plateau on a small patch of clear land. Normal access was by cable car to a station near the hotel. Three teams were readied for the rescue mission. The first two, a mixture of Student's airborne troops and Skorzeny's commandos, were assigned to the Gran Sasso operation. The third was tasked with freeing the Duce's family from house arrest in their country home.

Skorzeny and his men would not be arriving to snatch Mussolini by cable car. Twelve gliders, each capable of carrying ten troops, and their tugs were flown in from the South of France. H-hour was fixed for dawn on September 12. To minimise the risk of bloodshed, Skorzeny persuaded a senior Italian officer, General Soletti, to fly with him.

On the 12th the mission was delayed by bad weather and then an Allied bombing raid which cratered the runway. When the gliders eventually took off, two of them came to grief before they were airborne. Skorzeny, in the lead glider, was at his most forceful, shouting instructions to his pilot through a hole he had slashed in the canvas.

As Skorzeny's force made its final run-in to the plateau, it became clear that the triangle of open ground surrounding the hotel was not level but steeply sloped. Against Student's explicit instructions, Skorzeny ordered a crash landing.

His glider slithered to a halt only 30ft (9m) from the hotel. Skorzeny leapt out and hurtled past seemingly paralysed sentries through the front door. The wireless transmitter inside was swiftly put out of action before a signal could be sent, and amid scenes of complete chaos Mussolini was located on the first floor. Not a shot had been fired.

Even as he confronted the Duce, Skorzeny was distracted by the sight, through the window, of the last of his gliders plummeting into the side of the mountain as it was caught by a thermal. Firing could now be heard, and the senior Italian officer was summoned to order his men to surrender. He did so over a glass of wine.

By now the cable car had been secured and more Germans were arriving on the plateau. Skorzeny signalled Student that Mussolini was in their hands. But how was he to be extracted from the mountain-top hideaway?

The original plan had been to return to the valley below, where a Fiesler Storch light aircraft would be waiting. But this aircraft had been damaged while landing. There was only one thing for it. A second Fiesler Storch, circling the site as a spotter, would have to land on the plateau itself.

The Fiesler Storch got down to receive its passengers: Mussolini, looking haggard underneath an incongruous Homburg hat, scrambled into the rear seat and Skorzeny squashed into the passenger space behind. Take-off was nerve-racking — three up in a Storch and flying off the edge of a cliff. The overburdened aircraft slid into the air and then plunged downwards. The pilot, Captain Gerlach, regained control only 100ft (30m) from the valley floor.

They then flew on to Rome, where Mussolini and Skorzeny boarded an He 111 for Vienna. That night Hitler's daring commando was presented with the Knight's Cross, becoming the only man to be presented with the medal on the day he won it.

Far left; As Mussolini was escorted to the Fieseler Storch which would take him to Rome and thence to German-held northern Italy, he must have been reflecting upon his dubious form of freedom as Hitler's puppet.

BELOW LEFT: Skorzeny is personally congratulated by Adolf Hitler for the Mussolini rescue. In a later exploit, Skorzeny kidnapped the son of Hungarian dictator, Admiral Horthy, in October 1944, to prevent the conclusion of an armistice with the Russians. After the war Skorzeny lived in Spain and played an important but shadowy role in arms dealing and Cold War covert operations.

BELOW: Skorzeny towers over Mussolini as they await the arrival of the Fieseler Storch.

The Chindits Expeditions

ABOVE: Major-General Orde Wingate, one of the most colourful and controversial Allied commanders of the war, briefs his men at the Chindits' main base in Assam.

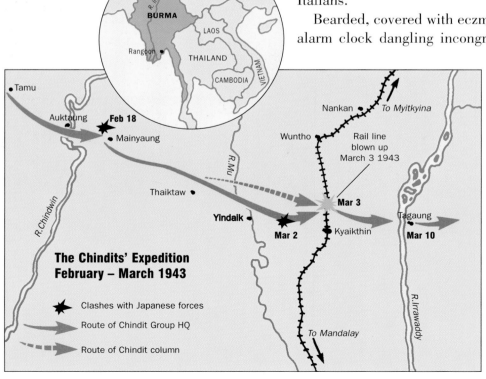

The Chindits' Expedition February – March 1943

★ Clashes with Japanese forces

➤ Route of Chindit Group HQ

➤ Route of Chindit column

On February 13 1943, British Army Brigadier Orde Wingate addressed the men under his command: 'Today we stand on the threshold of battle. The time of preparation is over, and we are moving on the enemy to prove ourselves and our methods. We need not, as we go forward into the conflict, suspect ourselves of selfish or interested motives. We have all had the opportunity of withdrawing and are here because we have chosen to bear the burden and the heat of the day.' Wingate was the commander of a force which became known as the Chindits, the long-range penetration group which he had formed for operations behind the Japanese lines in Burma. The name was taken from the Chindits' distinctive arm badge of a chinthe, or stone lion, which guarded the entrance to Burmese stone temples. The 40-year-old Wingate was one of the most remarkable commanders of the war. Born into a family of Plymouth Brethren, he had become an ardent Zionist and specialist in guerrilla warfare. In 1936, while serving in the British Army in Palestine, Wingate had organised Special Night Squads to combat Arab insurgents. In the 1940-41 campaign in Ethiopia, he commanded a mobile group, known as Gideon Force, which successfuly raised the local tribes against the Italians.

Bearded, covered with eczma and frequently to be seen with an alarm clock dangling incongruously from the belt of his battledress, Wingate was a massively eccentric figure who attracted as many enemies as admirers. Some thought him a genius, others a madman. Wingate compared himself with Napoleon. After a frustrating stint as a staff officer, during which he attempted suicide, Wingate arrived in India in 1942, where he was given the task of forming a small force of fast-moving guerrillas, supplied by air, who would take on the Japanese in their own element, the jungle.

The Chindits, officially designated 77th Indian Infantry

Brigade and comprising British, Gurkha and Burmese troops, underwent a period of gruelling training at Wingate's hands. By the beginning of February 1943, they were ready to conduct their first independent raid behind enemy lines.

Wingate divided his 3,250 men into two groups, each consisting of a number of columns of about 450 men and 100 mules. Detachments of RAF radio operators maintained contact with the aircraft tasked with dropping supplies. Each man carried some 60lb (27kg) of equipment, including rifle, bayonet, ammunition and grenades, water bottle, four pairs of socks, spare shirt, climbing rope, utility knife and and a five day ration pack, consisting of biscuits, cheese, nuts and raisins, dates, tea, sugar, milk and chocolate.

The smaller group, two columns strong and commanded by Lieutenant-Colonel Leigh Alexander, crossed the Chindwin River and struck south to attack the Mandalay-Myitkyina railway at Kyaikthin, 120 miles (190km) north of Mandalay. Wingate, accompanying the five columns led by Lieutenant-Colonel S. Cooke, planned to cut the same railway line between Wuntho and Indaw, to the north.

Wingate drove his men hard through the mountainous Burmese jungle, a series of seemingly endless green-clad ridges and valleys. In this pitiless environment, the Japanese were only one of the enemies which the Chindits would face. There was the torrential rain which produced seas of glutinous mud and permanently sodden clothes. Dense thickets of prickly bamboo slashed clothes and flesh to ribbons. Like Wingate, many of the Chindits wore beards which obviated the need for a shaving kit, provided good face camouflage in the jungle war of ambush and stalking, and kept out mosquitoes and ticks.

Progress was painfully slow but by the beginning of March Cooke's group was positioned to attack the railway. On March 2, the column led by Major Bernard Fergusson brushed aside a Japanese patrol and blew the

bridge at Bongyaung, the sound of the explosion rolling around the hills as Fergusson's mules kicked and plunged in panic.

The Japanese response was swift. Two divisions were despatched to deal with the intruders, whom the Japanese, unaware of the Chindits' air supply, believed to be on a reconnaissance rather than a raiding mission. The Japanese net closed in on the two Chindit groups, and a series of vicious close quarters engagements erupted in the jungle. One of Alexander's columns

ABOVE: Chindits man a mortar in the jungle, where it turned tree and bamboo splinters into deadly missiles.

TOP: A Chindit trooper carries an ill or wounded colleague to light transport for evacuation. Apart from vicious fighting, the Chindits suffered hunger and physical deprivation in the Burmese jungles.

and its headquarters were ambushed. Survival often depended on suprise. One night, Fergusson crept into a village and aproached four men sitting round a fire to ask its name. Only at the last moment did he realise they were Japanese. As they turned towards Fergusson, he tossed a grenade with a four-second fuse into the fire, killing them all.

Rather than withdraw, and jeopardise the Chindits' future, Wingate pressed deeper into enemy territory towards the Irrawaddy River, leaving his force two rivers to cross when they fell back to India. Wingate crossed the Irrawaddy on March 19 and linked up with the columns led by Fergusson and Major Michael 'Mad Mike' Calvert. But now the Chindits found themselves in heavily patrolled, open, waterless territory which was totally unsuited to guerrilla operations.

The commander of British IV Corps, Lieutenant-General Scoones, ordered Wingate to withdraw. Wingate in turn instructed both groups to disperse in small, independent parties. Alexander's group shifted to the east, hoping to reach the safety of China, while the northern group fell back on the Irrawaddy. The men were now exhausted and riddled with disease. The wounded had to be left behind. One of them, Lieutenant Philip Stibbe of Fergusson's column, later recalled his first night alone: 'As it grew dark I heard a lot of rustling in the leaves near where I lay and, to my horror, I saw several large spiders about the size of my hand crawling towards me. No doubt they were attracted by the smell of blood. It was a beastly sensation lying there unable to move while these loathsome creatures crawled nearer.' Stibbe was captured by the Japanese but survived the war.

One by one the small groups of Chindits completed the nightmarish return march to cross the Chindwin. Of the force which had set out nearly three months before, over 800 were lost, killed or wounded, many of them in the last stages of their march, where the Japanese lay in wait for them. Numbers of the survivors were so debilitated that they never saw combat again.

BELOW: A recalcitrant mule is manhandled on to a Dakota transport. Although Chindit columns were resupplied by airdrop, each had its own mule train.

On the face of it, the first Chindit campaign had not been a success. The Chindits had cut a few railway lines – which were quickly repaired – and killed several hundred Japanese. But they had achieved a tremendous psychological victory when it was needed most, taking the fight to the enemy and in the process undermining the myth of Japanese invincibilty in the jungle.

As a result, the Chindit force was expanded to six infantry

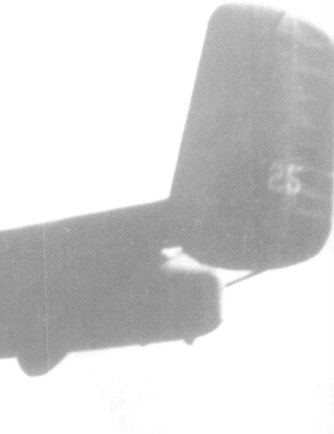

brigades totalling some 23,000 men. Wingate was promoted to Major-General and given a 'private air force' – 25 transports, 12 bombers, 30 fighters, 100 spotters and 225 gliders of the USAAF's No. 1 Air Commando.

In March 1944 the Chindits operated southwest of Myitkyina against the Japanese rear while the latter were conducting the U-go offensive against Imphal and Kohima. The air-supplied strongholds established by the Chindits tied down two and a half enemy divisions, but on the evening of March 24 Wingate was killed when the Mitchell bomber in which he was flying crashed into a hillside southwest of Imphal. Under their new commander, Brigadier William 'Joe' Lentaigne, the Chindits were then moved north to support General Stilwell's Chinese-American army whose advance on Myitkyina had been held-up by stubborn Japanese resistance.

By the second week in July the Chindits had reached the limit of their endurance. But the hardbitten 'Vinegar Joe' Stilwell, who had misused the lightly armed Chindits in assaults on heavily defended positions, a role for which they had not been trained, refused all requests to relieve them. Finally, he was sternly reminded by British Admiral Mountbatten, the Supreme Allied Commander South East Asia, 'If they are not soon relieved we may both be faced with the ... accusation of keeping men in battle who are unable to defend themselves.'

Stilwell chose to keep the remaining fit men on garrison duty, but by the end of August the rest of the Chindits had been flown out to India. Losses were 5,000 men. It can be argued that more was demanded of the Chindits than any other Allied troops in the war. They responded magnificently.

BELOW: A party of Chindit sappers lay charges to destroy a rail bridge, thus thwarting Japanese troop and equipment movement.

The Epic of the X-craft

ABOVE: Lieutenant B. C. G. Place (left) and Lieutenant D. Cameron pictured on their liberation from a POW camp near Bremen. Place and Cameron won VCs for their X-craft raid on the *Tirpitz*.

BELOW: A surfaced 'mother ship' tows an X-craft out to sea toward its target.

Lurking in Norwegian waters, the German battleship *Tirpitz* was known as the Lone Queen of the North, posing a constant threat to the Allied convoys to Russia. The British Prime Minister, Winston Churchill, had proposed attacking the Tirpitz in her base in 1942, but it was not until January 1943 that the Royal Navy took delivery of the weapon which was to be used against her – the midget submarine known as the X-craft.

The tiny X-craft, measuring only 51ft (15.5m) from stem to stern, had been specially designed to attack enemy shipping in defended harbours by releasing two time-fuzed charges, each containing two tons of high explosive, beneath the hull of the target vessel. The design also incorporated a watertight space – the 'wet and dry' – situated between the forward compartment and the control room which could be flooded to enable a diver to make underwater sorties against obstacles.

Training on the 12th Submarine Flotilla's prototype X-craft, *X-3* and *X-4*, was begun at the remote Loch Cairnbawn, where conditions closely resembled those their four-man crews would encounter in the Norwegian fjords. Net cutting and mock attacks on capital ships of the Home Fleet were the principal features of the preparation for the attack on *Tirpitz*, codenamed Operation 'Source'.

After the delivery of the first six production X-craft there was a long delay while they were worked up and the Admiralty waited for the return of the long northern nights to hinder detection by German coastal defences.

On September 9 1943, *Tirpitz* was photographed in Kaafjord by a Spitfire PR VII high-altitude reconnaissance aircraft flying from the Russian airbase at Vaenga. Two days later the six midget submarines set out from Loch Cairnbawn. The submarines *X-5*, *X-6* and *X-7* were to attack *Tirpitz*; *X-9* and *X-10*'s target was the battleship *Scharnhorst* berthed in Langefjord, as was the battleship *Lutzow*, the target of *X-8*.

On the first stage of their mission, the X-craft were towed by larger submarines travelling on the surface while the midget subs remained submerged at a depth of 50ft (15.5m). Two days out from the Norwegian coast the mother submarines submerged. All went smoothly until the early hours of the 15th when a heavy sea got up, pitching the cramped X-craft about in a series of sickening corkscrews.

Trouble struck when *X-8*'s towing cable snapped. She was eventually reunited with her mother ship, *Seanymph*, but was then forced to jetison her explosive charges, which were leaking. *X-8* was then damaged when the charges exploded and had to be scuttled. Then *X-9*'s towline to *Syrtis* snapped and she was never seen again.

At dusk on September 20 the towed X-craft reached their slipping zones at Soroy Island. The X-craft's passage crews had been replaced by their operational crews and now they began to thread their way through the coastal minefields. After their gruelling journey, the X-craft were beset by numerous problems. *X-10* was forced to jettison her charges and turn back. She was picked up by the submarine *Stubborn* and then scuttled. This left the three X-craft tasked with attacking *Tirpitz*.

On *X-6*, commanded by Lieutenant Donald Cameron, the automatic helmsman ('George') had broken down, the periscope had flooded and the submarine was listing ten degreees to starboard as a side charge began to take in water.

Nevertheless, at 4.15am on the 22nd, after hiding on the bottom during the daylight hours of the 21st, *X-6* dived to 60ft (18m) and set course fro *Tirpitz*.

By 7am, *X-6* had slipped through the gate in the floodlit antisubmarine net stretching across Kaafjord and was approaching the net protecting *Tirpitz*. Lieutenant Cameron screwed up his eyes as he raised and swivelled the periscope to make out the outline of the battleship in the sharp morning light.

Then there was a loud bang and a flash. The periscope's electric hoist motor had short-circuited and burst into flames. Cameron

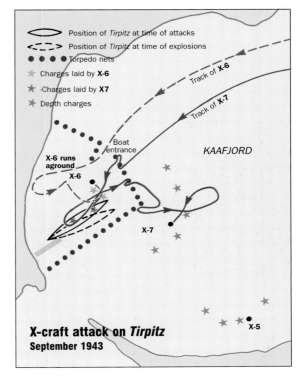

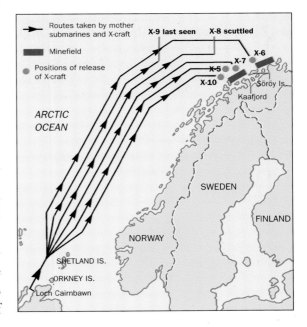

ABOVE: Guarded by massive shrouds of anti-submarine netting, *Tirpitz* lies at Kaafjord after her attack by the X-craft and air strikes.

dived and exstinguished the blaze before boldly following a harbour craft through a narrow gate which had been left in *Tirpitz*'s anti-torpedo net. Once through the net, Cameron dived for deeper water, then came up for a quick look at *Tirpitz* before diving again and heading for the battleship's stern.

Almost immediately there was a huge crash as *X-6* struck a large rock which bounced her up to the surface only a few yards from *Tirpitz*. Cameron dived again, only to become entangled with an obstruction under *Tirpitz*'s port bow. When *X-6* came up again, she was raked by small arms fire from the battleship. Cameron dived to place his charges below *Tirpitz*'s 'B' turret.

The game was now up for *X-6*, and Cameron surfaced, destroyed vital documents, opened his cocks and waited to surrender to a motor launch from *Tirpitz*. The time was 7.22am. On board the battleship, Cameron and his men underwent the uncomfortable experience of being interrogated while sitting on top of at least four tons of explosive which was about to detonate within minutes.

In fact there was more. *X-7*, commanded by Lieutenant Godfrey Place, had penetrated *Tirpitz*'s lair after spending an hour caught in an anti-torpedo net. After breaking free, *X-7* had surfaced bare-

RIGHT: A heavily camouflaged *Tirpitz*. Her only active operation of the war came in September 1943 when, escorted by ten destroyers, she bombarded shore installations at Spitzbergen.

ly 120ft (36m) from the battleship before diving to the bottom. Bumping around *Tirpitz*'s hull, Place laid one charge under 'A' turret and the second amidships. With her compass failing and air pressure falling, *X-7* was then ensnared in the net for a second time as she tried to escape.

At 8.12am the charges underneath *Tirpitz* exploded. The battleship was lifted clean out of the water and then crashed back, listing heavily to port, a hole torn in her hull, her rear gun turret ripped loose and with serious damage sustained by her engine, steering and damage-control systems.

One man had been killed and 40 injured, but Cameron and his crew had been no more than shaken. Rather more badly shaken were the men in *X-7*, which had been thrown clear of the net by the force of the charges detonating under *Tirpitz*.

Forced to the surface, *X-7* was met with a hail of fire from anti-aircraft guns. With bullets pinging off the hull Lt. Place made for a practice target and jumped to safety, waving a white flag. *X-7* sank to the bottom. Only one of Place's crew survived. Sub-Lieutenant Robert Aitken used *X-7*'s escape apparatus to appear on the surface after a desperate three-hour fight to save his comrades.

Mystery still surrounds the fate of *X-5*, commanded by Lieutenant Henty-Creer. Almost certainly, *X-5* was able to lay its charges under *Tirpitz*. At 8.43am she was seen surfacing beyond the torpedo net some 600 yards (550m) from the battleship. Hit by fire from the *Tirpitz*, *X-5* dived. German hydrophones picked up noises which suggested that Henty-Creer and his men were trying to repair her. But she was never seen again. In all probability, her fate was sealed by a depth charge.

Although none of the X-craft survived Operation Source, the attack on the *Tirpitz* had been a success. For the loss of nine men killed and six captured, *Tirpitz* had been disabled for six months. *Lutzow* was sent to safer waters, leaving only *Scharnhorst* at large in Arctic waters.

TOP: Sub-Lieutenant Aitken squeezing into the conning tower of *X-7*. Aitken won the DSO for his part in Operation Source.

ABOVE: The Crew of *X-7*: left to right, Aitken, Place, Sub-Lieutenant Whittam, and Lieutenant Peter Philip. Sitting, ratings Magennis and Luck (passenger crew) and the helmsman, Artificer Whiteley. Whittam and Whiteley died in the operation.

The Battle of Monte Cassino

ABOVE: One of the defenders of Monte Cassino with an FG42, a gas-operated rifle capable of single shots or automatic fire.

By the end of 1943 German forces in Italy had been shunted back to the Gustav defensive line, running from the Garigliano River estuary on the west coast, along the Rapido, to just south of Pescara on the Adriatic. This formidable network of defensive positions, barring the Allies' path to Rome and erected along the ribs which run east and west from Italy's mountainous spine, was held by the General von Vietinghoff's 10th Army under the overall command of the able Field Marshal Albert Kesselring, the German C-in-C in Italy.

In the middle of the Gustav Line stood a colossal chunk of rock called Monte Cassino, towering 1,700ft (520m) above the town below and crowned with an ancient Benedictine monastery guarding the Liri Valley and the road to Rome, only 75 miles (120km) away. Its strategic position had ensured that, since its founding in the 6th Century, the monastery had been destroyed and rebuilt four times.

Monte Cassino lay in the path of the US Fifth Army led by Lieutenant-General Mark Clark. The Allies decided to outflank the Gustav Line with an amphibious assault at Anzio, behind the

German lines, while simultaneously launching a frontal assault on Monte Cassino. Ironically, the Germans had not placed any troops in the monastery, The local corps commander, General Frido von Senger und Etterlin – who was a lay member of the Benedictine order – had forbidden it. He placed his defences, expertly camouflaged and manned by the elite 1st Parachute Division, in the crags and re-entrants of the mountain.

Clark launched his frontal attack on Monte Cassino on January 17 1944. The ensuing battle was to have a truly international flavour: in addition to the American Fifth Army and the British Eighth Army, Allied formations included a corps of French colonial troops, Canadians, New Zealanders, Poles, South Africans, Gurkhas and Rajputans from India and muleteers from Cyprus. To simplify logistics, the American-equipped divisions were grouped together, as were those equipped by the British.

The first attempt to break through the Gustav Line, mounted by the British X Corps, the US II Corps and the French Corps, broke down amid raging blizzards and strong German counter-attacks. By February 12 the Allies had been fought to a standstill. The US 34th Division had got to within a few hundred yards of Monte Cassino before being flung back.

Meanwhile the Allied force which had landed at Anzio found itself trapped on the beaches. Clark was now supplied with reinforcements by his superior, General Sir Harold Alexander, commander of 15th Army Group, who also harboured unjustified suspicions that the monastery had been incorporated into the German defences. Against Clark's vehement objections, Alexander ordered a bombardment of Monte Cassino after a warning to its monks to leave with the priceless art treasures it housed. The warning was in fact redundant, as

The Battle of Monte Cassino

← Allied advance
⬤⬤⬤ German fortified defensive line

Rome 70 miles/115km

Monte Cassino ▲ ⬤ Cassino
■ Station

FRONT LINE May 18

GUSTAV LINE

◁ Anzio 60 miles/95km

FRONT LINE Jan 17

BELOW: New Zealand infantry, using the ruins of Cassino as cover, work their way through the shattered town.

nearly all the monks had been evacuated by the Germans, and the art treasures removed, in the previous October.

On February 15 the attack began with an air strike by American bombers. An eyewitness recalled the start of the attack: 'There was a flash as might be expected from a giant striking titanic matches on the hillside. Then a pillar of smoke, 500ft (150m) high, hid the hill and hid the monastery from view. It was curiously beautiful, curiously sinister.' It was also a fatal error of judgement on the part of the Allies. Intact and undefended, the monastery was of no use to the Germans dug in on the slopes below it. When reduced to a landscape of craters and piles of rubble, Monte Cassino provided them with an almost impregnable fortress which they swiftly occupied.

The 2nd New Zealand and 4th Indian Divisions, commanded by General Sir Bernard Freyburg, the veteran of the Battle for Crete, failed to dislodge the German paratoops from their positions. The closest the British came to a breakthough was on the bitterly cold night of February 16 when a battalion of the Royal Sussex Regiment stormed Mount Calvario, a vital piece of high ground to the northwest of Cassino. But, at the moment when victory was within the British grasp, the Germans fired three green flares – the Sussex Regiment's signal to withraw. A subsequent attack by the Rajputans was beaten off.

In driving rain Freyburg's divisions attacked again on March 15 after an even heavier aerial bombardment. This only strengthened the German positions which were now honeycombed with bunkers and tunnels burrowed out of the rubble by the German paratroops. The lunar landscape made it impossible for the New Zealanders' armour to provide close support for the infantry, which could penetrate no farther than Cassino's shattered railway station.

On the peaks above, New Zealanders, Rajputana and Gurkhas

BACKGROUND PIC: The ruins of Monte Cassino, which provided its German defenders with perfect defensive positions.

BELOW: Poles load a mule on the outskirts of Cassino. The Poles were to play a gallant role in the closing phase of the battle.

fought bitter hand to hand battles for positions such as the ominously named Hangman's Hill, but Monte Cassino remained in German hands. Freyburg was forced to call off the attack on the 23rd.

The Allied response was to mount a fourth attack, preceded by a deception plan which convinced Kesselring that he faced another amphibious landing in his rear designed to cut off his line of retreat. Determined to crush Monte Cassino's defenders by sheer weight of numbers and firepower, Alexander assembled 14 divisions along a 20-mile (32km) front stretching from the mountains north of Cassino to the sea. The key to the plan was provided by the commander of the French Corps, General Alphonse Juin, who had persusaded Alexander that his North African troops, trained in the harsh conditions of the Atlas Mountains, could find a way through the mountains. This they did when, on May 11, the attack, codenamed Diadem, went in.

An hour before a pulverising bombardment made the very mountains seem to shake, Juin's 9,000 Goumiers, their equipment and ammunition carried by 4,000 mules, began infiltrating the 10,000ft (3,050m) Aurunci Mountains south of Cassino. They achieved complete surprise and within three days had burst into the Liri Valley. The path to Rome, along Route 6, now lay open.

The assault on Monte Cassino had been spearheaded by the 50,000 men of the Polish II Corps, led by General Wladyslaw Anders, who had begun his military career in World War I as an officer in the Russian Imperial Army. In September 1939, after the Red Army had entered Poland, Anders had been captured by the Russians and had spent two years in a Moscow prison. Now, however, Anders' sole aim, shared by his men, was to wreak revenge on the Germans who had occupied his homeland.

The Poles attacked on the morning of May 12 advancing over open ground behind a creeping barrage which provided them with their only cover. They fought for Monte Cassino for five days. On the 18th an eerie quiet descended over the battlefield. A scouting party of Lancers moved forward to discover a pathetic party of Germans too badly wounded to be moved from their positions. The monastery fortress had been abandoned.

The Lancers improvised a pennant from a Red Cross flag and a blue handkerchief and planted it amid the nightmarish shambles which was all that was left of the monastery. The four-month battle of Cassino had cost the Allies 21,000 casualties, including 4,100 killed. The Germans lost a similar number of men, many of whose bodies were never recovered from the rubble of Monte Cassino.

BOTTOM: A Sherman tank of US Fifth Army in action against snipers on April 8, a month before the start of the final battle for Monte Cassino.

BELOW: The fog of war: a German infantryman races between ramparts of rubble during an Allied bombardment.

The Marines at Wake Island

On December 7 1941, the Japanese entered the war, launching a devastating surprise attack on the great American naval base at Pearl Harbor on the Hawaiian island of Oahu. Neither the Americans nor the colonial powers in the Far East and Pacific were in any way prepared to stem the tide of Japanese conquest. For six months the Japanese ran riot, carving out a huge Pacific empire. By April 1942 the islands of Guam and Wake, the Philippines, French Indochina, Burma, Thailand, Malaya and the Dutch East Indies, three-quarters of New Guinea

BACKGROUND PIC: Wake was defended by a squadron of Marine Wildcats, the US Navy's standard fighter at the outbreak of the war in the Pacific. The Wildcat had a maximum speed of 375mph (600km/h) and was armed with six 0.50in machine-guns.

and Papua, the Bismarck archipelago and a substantial part of the Gilbert and Solomon Islands were in Japanese hands. To the north they threatened the Aleutians and the approaches to Alaska; in the west they were encamped on the border of India; to the south they threatened Australia.

In December 1941, the tiny atoll of Wake, lying some 2,000 miles (3,200km) west of Hawaii and consisting of three separate islets,, was held by a force of 450 US Marines and 75 Army Signals Corps and Navy personnel under the overall command of Commander W. Scott Cunningham. On Wake work was progressing on the construction of an airfield which would turn the atoll into a floating aircarft carrier. On December 7 the atoll came under heavy air attack which destroyed seven of Wake's squadron of 12 Wildcat fighters, commanded by Major Paul A. Putnam. Three days later a strong Japanese naval task force moved on Wake, comprising three light cruisers, six destroyers, two patrol boats, two medium transports and two submarines.

At 3am on December 11 Commander Cunningham was roused: Major James P. Devereux, the commander of the ground forces at Wake, had sighted ships on the horizon. They might be friendly but the likelihood was that they were Japanese. Help was too far away. To oppose a Japanese naval bombardment, the Marines had just six elderly 6in (152mm) guns in three batteries whose fire control systems had been rendered useless after the initial aerial bombardment. Cunningham decided to ambush the Japanese. No searchlights would be turned on. The garrison at Wake would wait in the dark until the last moment and then hit the Japanese with every-

BELOW: Men of the elite Japanese special landing forces who spearheaded Japan's Pacific drive in the first six months of the war.

ABOVE: A Japanese artist's impression of the surrender of the US Marines at Wake.

CHINA
Korea   JAPAN
Vietnam
PACIFIC
OCEAN

Wake   Midway Is.
Island

HAWAIIAN
Is.

PHILIPPINES   PACIFIC
OCEAN

Pearl
Harbor

PAPUA
NEW GUINEA

**The Marines at
Wake Island**

AUSTRALIA

thing they had. Cunningham later recalled: 'It was a perfect tropical night. A half moon was coming up over the ocean and the air was cool and soft. The roar of the surf had a soothing almost hypnotic quality about it.'

The Marines at Wake were now digging their foxholes deeper and awaiting the order to fire. Wake's four remaining Wildcat fighters stood ready on the attol's airstrip. By 5am the Japanese task force was within 5 miles (8km) of Wake, moving parallel to the atoll's southern shore. The Japanese carefully nosed their way in, laying down a preparatory bombardment. But it was not until just over an hour later that Cunningham ordered his guns to open fire. The second salvo from the gun at Peacock Point scored three direct hits on the light crusier *Yubari*, the flagship of the task force's commander, Admiral Kajioka. The cruiser turned and steamed away out of range. A second battery and then a third opened up, scoring a succession of hits on the task force's transports, another cruiser and two destroyers, one of which, *Hayate*, blew up and sank.

The Japanese task force withdrew under a heavy smokescreen, pursued by the Marines' Wildcats which had taken off when Devereux's batteries had opened fire. To their pilots' astonishment, the enemy had no air cover. The Wildcats bombed and strafed two light cruisers, set fire to a transport and sank the destroyer *Kisaragi* when a single bomb dropped by Captain Henry Elrod scored a direct hit on the depth charges stored on its afterdeck. The remnants of the Japanese task force limped away over the horizon.

In the opening exchange at Wake, the Japanese had lost two destroyers – the first Japanese ships to be sunk by the Americans in the war – and at least 500 men; the Marines had suffered only one fatal casualty. However, they had lost two of their precious Wildcats, one of which had crashlanded on Wake while the other had been disabled by flak. Both pilots had survived.

Admiral Kajioka withdrew to to Kwajalein in the Marshalls to ponder his next move. On Wake the Marines celebrated their remarkable victory. Cunningham recalled: 'It was like a fraternity picnic;. war whoops of joy split the air; warm beer was sprayed on late arrivals without regard to rank....'

The celebrations were shortlived. At 9am 17 Japanese bombers appeared over Wake. Fifteen flew away, two of them having been shot down by Lieutenant Davidson. Then the dead were buried – 26 officers and men of the fighter squadron and some 40 of the 1,500 civilians engaged on building the airfield.

Japanese bombers continued to pound Wake, and at 2am on December 23 a second, larger task force, under Admiral Kajioka, arrived off Wake. It was supported by six heavy cruisers and two of the aircraft carriers which had attacked Pearl Harbor, *Soryu* and

Hiryu. Some 2,000 Japanese Marines had been given the task of occupying Wake. Cunningham wrote that the fresh attack was launched 'in an atmosphere of desperate confusion from which only one clear factor emerged – the overwhelming numerical superiority of the invaders'.

The fight for Wake's three islets was savage. Some of the construction workers grabbed weapons and fought alongside the Marines. On one of the islets the beach was littered with the bodies of more than 100 Japanese Marines of the first wave. At daybreak, dive-bombers from the carriers screamed down on the American positions. The gallant Wildcats had gone, the last one disappearing while on patrol on the 22nd. The surviving pilots fought shoulder to shoulder with the Marines.

At 7.30am on the 24th the US Marines were still grimly hanging on, but the Japanese had clawed their way to within yards of the empty magazine on the largest islet which was being used as a makeshift hospital. With more than 1,000 unprotected civilians on the island, Cunningham wanted to avoid a massacre. He decided to surrender, ordered his men to destroy their weapons and hoisted a white sheet over his command post. In the defence of Wake 122 men had died.

Ironically, two weeks before the final assault on Wake began, a US naval task force had been prepared to reinforce the atoll. It had included the carrier *Saratoga*, with its 72 fighters and dive-bombers, but the task force was recalled before *Saratoga* had got within range of Wake. After the heavy losses sustained at Pearl Harbor, Admiral William Pye, acting commander of the Pacific Fleet, was reluctant to risk one of his major assets. A seaplane tender was sent ahead of *Saratoga* to evacuate Wake but this ship, too, was recalled. The men on Wake were left to fight alone.

ABOVE: Battered Wildcats at Wake testify to the battle for the atoll. The fighters which survived the first Japanese assault inflicted damage on the enemy which was out of all proportion to their numbers.

BELOW: An aerial view of Wake in 1944 when this time it was under attack from Allied bombers which have raised a pall of smoke from Japanese installations.

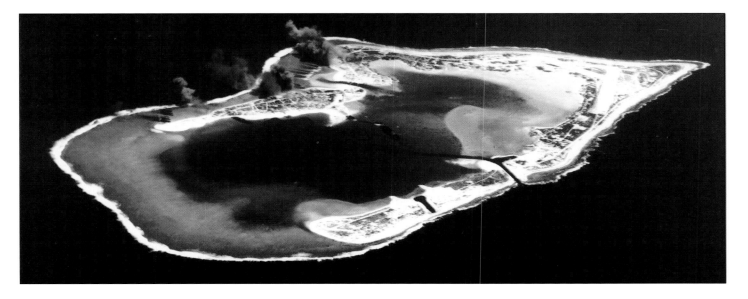

The Heroes of Kohima

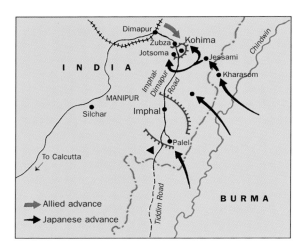

ABOVE: A British mortar in action at Kohima. In the jungle, the platoon or company mortar was a deadly weapon.

On March 6 1944, the Japanese launched the 'U-go' offensive in northern Burma. U-go had twin aims: to pre-empt the Allies' own plans to retake Burma; and to break into India itself.

The failure of successive British offensives in the Arakan, the steamy coastal region from which it was hoped it would be possible to gain access to central Burma, had reinforced the Japanese high command's low opinion of their opponents' abilities as jungle fighters. They were confident of victory, but were soon to be taught a terrible lesson.

The gateway to India lay through the isolated border town of Imphal in the then district of Manipur. A 130-mile (210km) road wound north from Imphal to the hill town of Kohima before running on to the railhead at Dimapur. It was Kohima's only contact with the outside world and would link the two remote settlements in the high hills of Assam in some of the most savage fighting of the war.

Two divisions of the Japanese 15th Army, commanded by the hot-tempered General Renya Mutaguchi, crossed the Chindwin River and moved on Imphal. The third headed for Kohima. Both the Japanese and the British were operating under severe disadvantages. Time was not on Mutaguchi's side. Once battle was joined, his troops could rely on no more than a month's supplies. In May, the monsoon would arrive, making offensive operations all but impossible. In contrast, the commander of the British 14th Army, General William Slim, had been preparing to go over to the offensive and was not best placed to receive an attack in a sector where there were such poor communications and few facilities for the basing of the large numbers of troops now committed to the front.

Nevertheless, Slim had one invaluable advantage. Under his superb leadership, Fourteenth Army had been transformed from the shattered force which had been driven out of Burma in the spring of 1942 into a highly motivated army. But it had yet to fight a full-scale battle against experienced Japanese troops who had been ordered by the super-aggressive Mutaguchi to fight to the death.

The British were prepared for the Japanese thrust. Ample evidence of the build-up was provided by aerial reconnaissance. Nevertheless, Slim was surprised by its initial speed. By April 5 the Japanese had cut the Imphal-Kohima road and isolated both settlements. Slim ordered his subordinate commanders not to withdraw without permission from higher authority. It was imperative to deny the Japanese the mountain roads which led down into the Indian plain. Imphal and Kohima, the latter situated on a saddle ridge which in happier days was bright with forests of tropical flowers, would have to be held at all costs.

At Kohima, last-minute reinforcements were rushed in from Dimapur by the commander of the British XXXIII Corps, Lieutenant-General Montagu Stopford. Two battalions, supported by artillery, were positioned 2 miles (3km) west of Kohima while the third, the 4th West Kents, were placed in Kohima itself on the highest hill in the ridge, later to become known as Garrison Hill.

Fighting began on the 30th as General Sato's 31st Division pushed back the scattered units of the Assam Rifles and other regiments which were defending the approaches to Kohima. The commander at Kohima, Colonel Hugh Richards, had a force of approximately 1,200 men to resist the all-out attack of 12,000 Japanese jungle veterans. He had to rely on the arrival of a breakthrough force from Dimapur, the British 2nd Division, without which his defences would be overwhelmed.

The Japanese arrived on April 5. In the teeth of desperate resistance, they took the strongpoints on the hills and hummocks around Kohima. The pattern of the battle was now set. Men crouched in slit trenches sometimes only yards away from the enemy. One officer of the West Kents calculated that from the plop of a grenade being fired to its arrival was no more than 14 seconds. The intensity of Japanese artillery, mortar and sniper fire in such a small space meant that movement between units was virtually impossible by day and extremely hazardous at night. Few of the men locked in this fight for survival had a clear idea of what was happening beyond the lip of their own trench.

Day and night the British and Indian troops were subjected to Japanese broadcast appeals to them to surrender. Sato's aim was to

BOTTOM: Japanese troops advance with fixed bayonets towards the British defensive positions at Kohima.

BELOW: A view of the battle-scarred terrain at Garrison Hill which recalls the strips of murdered nature at the front in the First World War.

exhaust the defenders of Kohima. Japanese artillery was most active at dawn and sunset, shredding nerves as well as destroying targets. When darkness fell, the Allied troops stood to in the dark before the moon rose, straining to catch the rustle of Japanese infiltrators moving behind them. As one of Kohima's defenders observed, this stoked the fear that when he awoke the occupants of the next gunpit might be the enemy.

On April 11 Stopford sent 5th British Infantry Brigade up the Dimapur-Kohima road. Two days later it had smashed its way through to the Jotsoma 'box' held by 161st Brigade. By now, the situation at Kohima was desperate. A message was sent to 5th Brigade that unless help arrived within 48 hours Kohima would fall: 'The men's spirits are all right but there aren't many of us left....'

On the 17th the Japanese launched their fiercest attack on the slopes of Garrison Hill. Phosphorous bombardments were followed by howling infantry assaults with grenades and machine-guns. To the din was added the fire of the defenders' howitzers. By the night of the 18th the men holding Garrison Hill were on their last legs. One young private asked Colonel Richards, 'When we die, sir, is that the end or do we go on?'

The Japanese swarmed everywhere but were unable to mount a co-ordinated battalion-strength attack which would have spelled the end at Kohima. The ground around Garrison Hill – just 350 yards (320m) square – was now all that was left of the perimeter which had been held on April 5. But the men of the West Kents hung on until dawn on the 20th when troops of the Royal Berkshires, the advance guard of 2nd Division, broke in to relieve them. The stench of rotting corpses was so thick on Garrison Hill that many of the Berkshires were physically sick as they dug in on the battle-scarred hill, whose blasted trees were festooned with blackened shreds of the parachutes used in the air supply of the Kohima garrison.

The evacuation of the West Kents did not mean the end of the battle. The Japanese still occupied most of the Kohima massif and would have to be driven off amid the downpours of the monsoon, which brought with it mud, malaria and dysentery.

BELOW: Infantry clear caved-in Japanese bunkers on Scraggy Hill, captured by 10th Gurkha Rifles in fierce fighting in the Shenam area.

The most savage fighting of the battle erupted in mid-May. The sliver of ground at stake was the British Deputy Commissioner's bungalow and its adjcent tennis court. This had been seized on April 9 by the Japanese, who had built a warren of bunkers and weapons pits on the surrounding terraced hillsides. The task of winkling out the Japanese was given to the men of the 2nd Battalion Dorsetshire Regiment. It was a dirty business made more dificult by the terrain which denied the Dorsets any armoured support. A solution was found by the Royal Engineers who cut a path to a spur behind the bungalow. They then winched a Grant tank up and pushed it down the slope. It came to rest on the baseline of the tennis court, where its commander, Sergeant Waterhouse of the 149 Royal Tank Regiment poured a hail of fire into the Japanese bunkers at no more than 20 yards (18m) range.

The Japanese fled on to the waiting rifles of the Dorsets. Only the chimney stack of the bungalow remained. The rest of the landscape around was a shell-churned rubbish dump alive with rats. Whe he saw it, General Stopford compared it with the Somme in 1916: 'One could tell how desperate the fighting had been.'

By now the Japanese had run out of time, supplies and ammunition. On May 31, Sato ordered his men to withdraw to Imphal. Exhausted and riddled with disease, they were harried all the way by the Allies. Imphal was relieved on June 22, after over 80 days of siege, and now it was the turn of Mutaguchi to throw in the towel. Early in July, his 15th Army pulled out, the survivors struggling down liquefied roads to cross the Chindwin on to the Burma plains. Only 20,000 of the 85,000 Japanese who had come to invade India were left standing.

Slim now had a springboard for the reconquest of Burma. The cost to the Allies had been 17,587 British and Indian troops killed, wounded and missing. The dead at Kohima have their own simple and moving monument which bears the epitaph: 'When you go home, tell them of us, and say: "For your tomorrow, we gave our today".'

ABOVE: British infantry advance cautiously through long grass covered by a Bren gun, a standard light machine gun used by British and Commonwealth troops from 1936.

TOP: Infantry and armour of Stopford's XXXIII Corps move along the Kohima-Imphal road.

Darby's Rangers in Tunisia

ABOVE: Colonel William Darby astride a motorcycle in Tunisia in 1942. Although trained as an artilleryman, Darby proved highly effective as a trainer and motivator of elite infantry units.

The US Army Rangers were volunteer units formed to play the same role as the British Commandos. The first Ranger battalion completed its training at the Commando Training Centre at Achnacarry in Scotland in 1942. It comprised six companies, each consisting of three officers and 64 men drawn from every branch of the US Army. The companies were divided into two platoons, each of two asssault sections and a mortar section.

The original aim of the Rangers was to provide its wide range of men with combat experience in commando operations, then the only way of engaging the enemy on the European mainland. The men would return to their units to provide backbone for the heavy conventional fighting which would follow the invasion of northwest Europe. A small group of Rangers participated in the Dieppe raid in August 1942.

The man tasked with forming and training the first Ranger battalion was Colonel William Darby, a 31-year-old West Point-trained artilleryman and a super-fit disciplinarian. Darby's relentless training regime ensured that his Rangers were as tough and as highly motivated as any Commandos. Darby had placed particular emphasis on night fighting techniques, devising his own signalling method using red and green flashlights masked to emit only a pinpoint of light. In this way Darby's men could maintain formation while advancing, and he could control the operation by radio from the rear.

However, toward the end of 1942, the Rangers were beginning to suffer an identity crisis. The US Army had abandoned its idea of using the formation as a forcing bed for elite troops to stiffen less experienced units, and seemed unsure of how to use Darby's men. North Africa was to provide the answer.

The Rangers took part in Operation Torch, the Allied invasion of North Africa, seizing the port of Arzew, Algeria, in an amphibious night attack on November 7 1942. Then they were forced to kick their heels for several months while the Allies fought their way eastward against stiff Axis opposition.

It was not until February 1943 that a mission was found which was ideally suited to the Rangers' skills in night attack. In Tunisia, the Sened Pass, some 20 miles (32km) from the Allies' forward positions, carried the main road through central Tunisia to the coastal town of Sfax. It was defended by Italian Bersaglieri mountain troops and German armour. The Rangers were ordered to mount a lightning raid on this important Axis strongpoint, which was reconnoitred by Darby and his executive officer Major Herman W. Dammer.

The Rangers' jumping-off point was the oasis town of Gafsa on the southern edge of the Allied battle line. On the night of February 10, the three Ranger companies chosen for the mission set off by truck from Gafsa to join Darby and Dammer at a French outpost 25 miles (40km) to the east. On arrival, they immediately formed up and set off on a punishing speed march through mountainous terrain.

At first light the Rangers lay up in a hollow between two peaks about 6 miles (10km) from the Sened Pass. They spent the day huddled under their groundsheets in positions carefully camouflaged against enemy aircraft, while German armoured patrols rumbled over the plain below them.

As evening approached, the Rangers' section leaders were given their final briefing. There were three Italian strongpoints on the line of hills in front of the Pass. Each would be hit by a single company, A on the left, E in the centre and F on the right. When darkness fell, the Ranger column moved down into the plain. Under their balaclavas – they wore no helmets – their faces were blackened. At 2am on the 12th the column split up into its attack

ABOVE: Men of the Italian Bersaglieri in North Africa. These tough mountain troops acquitted themselves well in the Western Desert.

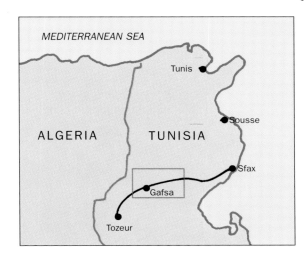

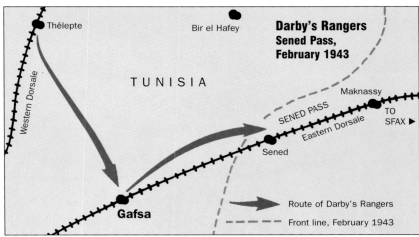

formations. Darby's signalling drill ensured that each of the companies approached in formation to within 300 yards (275m) of the enemy positions in complete silence and without being spotted.

It was only then that machine-gun fire split the night, quickly followed by the crump of 47mm cannon shells. The Rangers

BELOW: The Rangers took part in the Torch landings in November 1942. Heavy fighting lay ahead in Tunisia before the Allies secured the coast of North Africa.

RIGHT: Beach party: the Americans come ashore in North Africa in November 1942.

ABOVE: Battle-hardened veterans of the Afrika Korps man an observation post in a Tunisian village held by a regiment of panzergrenadiers.

hugged the earth, crawling forward and grimly obeying their own orders not to open fire until the last moment. They were so close that ahead of them they could hear excited Italian voices. Around them they could hear the cries of their own wounded.

After seeking brief safety behind the rise which lay in front of the enemy positions, the Rangers rose as one to charge the last few yards, hurling grenades and blazing away at the Italian machine-gunners with their Thompson guns. Behind them the mortar sections opened up on the Italian vehicle park.

Now they were at close quarters with the enemy. In the confined space of trenches the commando knives went to work. The ferocity and impetus of the assault overwhelmed the enemy. With resistance at an end, charges were placed against the troublesome artillery and the Rangers' wounded were attended to at makeshift medical posts.

With just over two hours to go before dawn, Darby ordered a withdrawal in two columns: the first consisted of the able-bodied under Dammer; the second, led by Darby, was made up of the wounded, some of them carried on stretchers improvised from groundsheets, Italian prisoners (vital for intelligence) and volunteers to aid and guard them. If they could not cover the 20 miles (32km) back to the outpost by daybreak, the men in the second column would be in danger of interception by the enemy.

Urged on by Darby, who himself took turns in carrying the stretchers, the column covered 14 miles (22km) of rugged terrain by daybreak. Now the morning sun illuminated their exhausted progress across the harsh plain. Then Darby's men were intercepted, not by German armour, however, but by a British armoured car sent out to cover their withdrawal.

After suffering a heavy bombing raid on Gafsa which greeted their arrival, the Rangers took stock. They had lost one man killed and suffered 18 wounded, but had killed at least 100 Italians and destroyed six of their cannon and 12 machine guns.

In the summer of 1943 Darby's command was expanded to three battalions, collectively known as Darby's Rangers. They fought in Sicily and at Salerno, and in the bitter slog through Italy. As the Ranger Force, they spearheaded the landings at Anzio in January 1944, but shortly afterwards two of Darby's battalions were all but wiped out when they were encircled by a superior German force near Cisterna.

Swordfish at Taranto

ABOVE: A Swordfish torpedo plane climbs away from a British carrier.

BELOW: The 'Stringbag', which could carry a single torpedo or mine or up to 1,100lb (500kg) of bombs, or eight rocket launchers. Defensive armament was provided by two machine guns.

T he year of 1940 was a dismal one for Britain. After the fiasco in Norway, the British Expeditionary Force had been bundled out of France. The gloom was relieved by the narrow margin achieved over the Luftwaffe in the Battle of Britain, but after the summer of 1940 Londoners and the inhabitants of Britain's major ports and industrial cities were enduring the Blitz.

But at the end of the year there occurred an event which not only boosted morale but also had a dramatic effect on the course of World War II. In Operation Judgement, carrier-based torpedo-bombers of the Fleet Air Arm destroyed the better part of the Italian Fleet at anchor in the naval base at Taranto, situated off the Ionian Coast of southern Italy. It was an operation whose origins lay in a 1938 plan devised by the Royal Navy's commander in the Mediterranean, Admiral Sir Dudley Pound. The plan became reality after Italy entered the war in June 1940. To the overstretched Mediterranean Fleet, the Italian Navy, whose main units were four operational battleships and seven heavy cruisers, presented a formidable threat. However, the Italian naval high command was determined not to risk its principal assets and so avoided a major confrontation with the outnumbered Royal Navy, which nevertheless possessed not only the advantage of greater operational experience but also had aircraft carriers.

The aggressive Admiral Sir Andrew Cunningham, commander of the Mediterranean Fleet from 1939, decided to use his carriers, the elderly *Eagle* and the newly commissioned *Illustrious* which had arrived in the theatre in September, to strike at the base at Taranto. The harbour was heavily defended by anti-aircraft guns and clusters of barrage balloons. The Italian battleships were cocooned by anti-submarine netting. There were no night fighters in the area, and it was decided that the attack would be launched under the cover of darkness.

The weapon for the task was the Fairey Swordfish, an open-cockpit biplane nicknamed the 'Stringbag' which had entered service in 1936 but already looked like an aircraft from a bygone age. In fact Swordfish were to serve the Fleet Air Arm with distinction until 1945. The lumbering, lightly armed biplane had a maximum speed of only 140mph (225km/h),

but it was highly manoeuvrable, and its canvas construction made capable of absorbing heavy punishment and easy to repair.

The date originally chosen for Judgement by Cunningham was October 21 1940 – Trafalgar Day – but a fire in *Illustrious*'s hangar caused its postponement. Then it became clear that *Eagle*, which had been struck by bombs in July, was badly in need of extensive repairs. The decision was taken to transfer five of *Eagle*'s Swordfish to *Illustrious*.

Illustrious sailed from Alexandria on November 6, accompanied by four battleships, *Warspite*, *Valiant*, *Malaya* and *Ramillies*, and screened by destroyers and cruisers. When she set sail she had 24 Swordfish on board, but three planes had to be ditched in the sea when it was found that their fuel tanks had been contaminated by water. There were now 21 aircraft to fly the mission, the crews being drawn from the Fleet Air Arm's 813, 815, 819 and 824 Squadrons.

The attack was planned to be delivered in two stages with an hour between them. The first wave, led by Lieutenant-Commander K. 'Hooch' Williamson, would comprise 12 Swordfish. Six of them would carry MkXII torpedoes, fitted with detonators which would be activated by a ship's magnetic field. Their task was to attack the battleships. Two Swordfish would carry flares to illuminate the targets, plus four 250lb (113kg) bombs, and the remaining four planes were armed with six bombs apiece. Their orders were to attack the harbour's oil facilities.

The second wave of nine Swordfish were led by Lieutenant-Commander 'Ginger' Hale. Its five torpedo-carriers were to get in among the battleships. None of the torpedo-carriers in both waves was assigned a specific target. It was hoped that in the confined space of Taranto's 'battleship row' a torpedo that missed one warship would run on to strike another.

In the late afternoon of November 10, *Illustrious* and her escorts left the main force and steamed towards the launching point off the island of Cephalonia, 160 miles (250km) from Taranto. At 8.30pm on the 11th, the first wave took off from the carrier, climbing to 7,000ft (2,130m) before droning northwestward laden with extra fuel and below a quarter moon. Williamson quickly realised that four of his Swordfish had become detached, but as the torpedo-bombers did not carry plane-to-plane radios, there was no way of regrouping his flight. The four Swordfish would have to find their own way to Taranto.

One which did was the Swordfish piloted by Lieutenant H.I. Swayne, who arrived over Taranto some 20 minutes ahead of time. Swayne decided to fly back and forth to wait for his comrades, in the process exciting the attention of the Italian gunners below, who were on full alert. The element of surprise on which Cunningham had counted had been sacrificed.

The lone Swordfish provoked a storm of fire not only from the guns ashore but the warships in the harbour. The sight which greeted the first wave as it flew in at 10.50pm was later recalled

BELOW: The Italian battleship *Conte di Cavour*, launched in 1910, rebuilt in the mid-1930s – and torpedoed by Swordfish in 1940.

by one of the marker pilots, Lieutenant Charles Lamb: '... before the first Swordfish dived to the attack, the full-throated roar from the guns of six battleships and the blast from the cruisers and destroyers made the harbour defences seem like a sideshow; they were the lunatic fringe, no more than the outer petals of the flower of flame which was hurtled across the water in wave after wave by a hot-blooded race of defenders in an intense fury of agitation, raging at a target they could only glimpse for fleeting seconds.'

While the marker planes illuminated the shore of the outer harbour, Williamson was the first to fly in, skidding past a balloon cable and a destroyer firing at pointblank range, to release his torpedo at the battleship *Conte di Cavour* from a height of 30ft (9m). As Williamson banked sharply, his Swordfish was raked by machine-gun fire and plunged into the harbour. Miraculously, Williamson and his observer, Lieutenant N.J. 'Blood' Scarlett, survived the crash, and a roughing up by angry Italian dockers, to be taken prisoner. The next battleship to be hit was *Littorio*, which had a 50ft (15m) gash opened in her starboard bow by Lieutenant N.M. Kemp. Lieutenant Swayne, who had started all the commotion, made amends by slamming a second torpedo into *Littorio*, which began to settle nose first into the harbour mud. After a hair-raising approach the last of the torpedo carriers, flown by Lieutenant M.R. Maund, got in a shot at the stricken battleship but scored only a glancing blow. At one moment Maund found himself barely 50 yards (45m) from the pom poms of a destroyer whose gunners were so startled that they did not fire until he was past them, zigzagging along just above the water.

Far to the south, the second wave was experiencing problems. On the deck of *Illustrious* two Swordfish locked together. When they were untangled, the plane piloted by Lieutenant E.W. Clifford was thought too badly damaged to fly and was sent below. The remaining eight took off but the other Swordfish involved in the incident was forced to turn back.

At about midnight 'Ginger' Hale led his seven Swordfish in, diving from 5,000ft (1,525m) to 30ft (9m) to release his torpedo against *Littorio* at a range of 700 yards (640m), blowing a hole in the bottom of her hull. Skimming over the water, Lieutenant C.S.C. Lea found the battleship *Duilio* filling his sights. His torpedo ran straight and true to strike her 30ft (9m) below the waterline. As the water cascaded in, *Duilio* was beached.

After narrowly missing a runaway barrage balloon, Lieutenant J.W.G. Welham's Swordfish was hit by anti-aircraft fire. Fighting with the controls, Welham roared in to release his torpedo at the

BELOW: One of the heroes of Taranto, Lieutenant E. W. Clifford, last of the Swordfish pilots to take off.

massive bulk of *Vittorio Veneto*. At this point Welham was flying well below the hail of flak, but with the release of the Mk XII his Swordfish bounced up into the worst of it. It seemed to Welham that every gun in Taranto was firing at him as he weaved his way to safety.

The last man in was the indomitable Lieutenant Clifford, who had bullied his fitters into repairing his damaged Swordfish in less than half an hour. After circling over the blazing harbour, Clifford chose to attack the cruiser *Trento*, moored in the inner harbour, with his six bombs. He scored one direct hit but the bomb failed to detonate.

Rendezvous time with *Illustrious* was 1am. At the agreed position, the carrier came up into the wind and put on steam for 21 knots. But the sky remained empty and radar screen blank. It was not until 1.20pm that the first Swordfish touched down. One by one they came in. After Lieutenant Welham had made a bumpy landing, he discovered that his port aileron rod had been wrecked; a yawning hole in the port lower mainlane revealed the remains of several shattered wing ribs. It was tribute both to Welham's airmanship and the robust qualities of the Swordfish that they had returned to *Illustrious* at all.

'None of us thought we would come out of it alive,' said one of the Swordfish crew later. Certainly Admiral Lyster in *Illustrious* had allowed for at least 50 per cent casualties. But in fact only two Swordfish were lost. Williamson and Scarlett survived but the other crew perished. Twenty biplanes had put three battleships out of action, one permanently and the others for several months. The same night British cruisers sank three Italian ships heading for Brindisi.

The Taranto raid not only altered the balance of power in the Mediterranean but also had a powerful strategic effect on the other side of the world. The C-in-C of the Japanese Combined Fleet, Admiral Yamamoto, keenly studied the results of the strike at Taranto, even despatching a team to Italy to take a first-hand look at the devastation. What Yamamoto learned was put to deadly effect a year later at Pearl Harbor.

ABOVE: The inner harbour at Taranto. In the top right-hand corner of this aerial reconnaissance photograph, damaged Italian cruisers can be seen disgorging oil into the water. The attack on Taranto was later used by the Japanese as a model for the pre-emptive strike at Pearl Harbor.

TOP: A Swordfish's wings are folded on the flight deck of the carrier *Illustrious*.

The Cherkassy Break-out

ABOVE: An officer of SS Panzer Division Wiking, a Pour le Merite at his neck, reads a letter from home in 1944. Established in the winter of 1940, Wiking contained, in addition to native Germans, men recruited from Norway, Denmark, the Low Countries and Estonia. After the battle of the Cherkassy pocket, in March 1944, the remnants of the division were sent to Poland to rest and refit. It later fought in Poland and then in Hungary in the abortive attempt to relieve Budapest. Wiking surrendered in Czechoslovakia in May 1945.

ABOVE RIGHT: A Red Army T-34, the best all-round tank of the war, which has tumbled into a trench system during the winter fighting in 1944.

At the beginning of 1944 six divisions of the German Army Group South – some 56,000 men of XI and XLII Corps – were encircled by the Russian Army in a pocket 30 miles (48km) wide and 20 (32) deep around the the souhwestern Ukrainian town of Korsun. The Germans referred to it as the 'Cherkassy pocket', after the nearby town of Cherkassy which straddled the River Dnieper.

At dawn on January 24, with the encirclement all but complete, the Red Army went on to the attack. General Konev's Second Ukrainian Front (the Russian equivalent of a German Army Group) took the lead. After a massive artillery bombardment, advanced battalions of 4th Guards and 53rd Armies had broken into the German forward positions to a depth of 3 miles (5km). The following day Konev threw in more infantry attacks before unleashing the Fifth Guards Tank Army, an elite formation commanded by the highly capable General Pavel Rotmistrov, in an attack at the base of the pocket. Rotmistrov's attack was halted by furious anti-tank fire, but the next day the attack was renewed from the north by General Vatutin's First Ukrainian Front led by the newly formed Sixth Guards Tank Army under General Kravchenko.

By the end of January the Russians had established an outer and inner encirclement of the Cherkassy pocket. The outer encirclement was entrusted to Fifth Guards and Sixth Tank Armies, reinforced with rifle divisions and standing ready to beat off the tanks of III and XLVII Panzer Corps which were trying to batter their way to the relief of the divisions trapped in the pocket.

Inside the pocket, conditions were rapidly deteriorating. Although the area in which the Germans were trapped was dotted with small villages and woodland, most of it was marshland, cut by ravines, streams and tributaries of the Dnieper. A sudden thaw had turned the entire area into a sea of mud, making its few roads impassable. Air supply of the pocket was all but impossible since the landing zones had been washed away. Ammunition and petrol were in short supply. The defenders of the pocket's perimeter were subjected to a ceaseless propaganda barrage by the Red Army, which employed captured German generals to broadcast appeals to their former comrades to surrender.

Now the Soviet forces began to launch concentric attacks against the pocket, slicing their way forward and harrying German units as they buckled, broke up and withdrew within the shrinking perimeter. The fighting in the Korsun pocket was as brutal as any on the Eastern Front. As scattered elements of a Belgian SS formation, the Wallonian Brigade, approached the village of Moshny, they encountered a furious battle raging around a German artillery battery, which was firing pointblank at waves of Red Army infantry. Flames leapt from the settlement's primitive buildings as, amid a mud-clogged mass of anti-aircraft guns, abandoned trucks and field kitchens, drivers, cooks, radio operators and quartermasters fought for their lives.

By February 12 four German panzer divisions were threatening to hack their way through the outer screen held by the Russian Sixth Tank Army while the divisions inside the pocket were trying deperately to join hands with them at the southwest corner of the pocket. Up till now Soviet bombers and ground-attack aircraft had had a field day against the columns of German armour and trucks crawling through the mud below them. But now the snows returned to ground the Red Air Force.

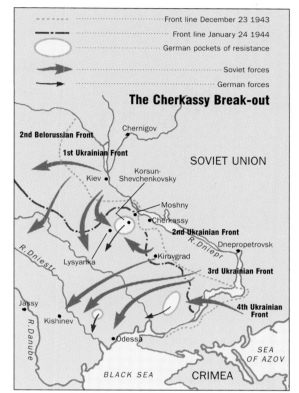

The Cherkassy Break-out

- Front line December 23 1943
- Front line January 24 1944
- German pockets of resistance
- Soviet forces
- German forces

2nd Belorussian Front
Chernigov
1st Ukrainian Front
SOVIET UNION
Kiev
Korsun-Shevchenkovsky
Moshny
Cherkassy
2nd Ukrainian Front
Dnepropetrovsk
R. Dniepr
R. Dniestr
Lysyanka
Kirovgrad
3rd Ukrainian Front
Jassy
4th Ukrainian Front
R. Danube
Kishinev
Odessa
SEA OF AZOV
BLACK SEA
CRIMEA

BELOW: German troops slog through the mud as the pressure mounts in the pocket. Campaigning in Russia was dominated by the 'rasputitsa' when the ground was turned into a sea of mud by either late-summer heavy rain or the end-of winter thaw.

ABOVE: Panzergrenadiers in winter camouflage smocks and MkIV tanks of Wiking Division prepare to break out of the pocket. The fight for survival at Korsun pushed these tough troops to the limit of their endurance.

RIGHT: German troops on the Eastern Front contemplate the grim face of 'General Winter'. The savage climate, for which the German Army in the East was at first unprepared, was traditionally one of the Red Army's principal weapons.

Nevertheless, by February 15 the pocket had been reduced to an area of about 35 square miles (90 sq km). Of the men crammed inside, only about one-third were combat troops. They had no shelter, and were exhausted and caked with mud and grime. The commander of XI Corps, General Stemmermann, was now frantically trying to organise his best fighting units, which included the SS Panzer division 'Wiking', into a breakout force to the west, through Lysyanka, towards III Panzer Corps.

Stemmermann ordered the destruction of all vehicles except

tanks, self-propelled guns, tracked vehicles and enough horse-drawn wagons to carry the wounded. The breakout, organised in two columns, was launched just before midnight on February 16. Snowstorms raged as Stemmermann's columns moved off.

Waiting for them were two Soviet armies, 27th and 4th Guards. At first all seemed to be going well for the Germans, but then the breakout began to collapse in chaos. Enfilading fire forced Wiking Division's panzergrenadier regiment to turn south to cross an icy 50ft (15m) wide river, the Gniloy Tich, in which hundreds of men drowned. Emerging into open country, the columns behind Wiking were set upon by Soviet tanks and Cossack cavalry. The men who raised their hands in surrender to the Cossacks had them sliced off by sabres glinting in the yellow early morning sky. On the banks of the Gniloy Tich, troops struggling to cross the river were pounded by Soviet arillery as Soviet tanks took them in the flanks and rear. By noon, SS Division Wiking had disintegrated. Its men abandoned their weapons to leap into the river, their only means of escape.

Some 6,000 men of the SS Panzer Division Wiking escaped from the Korsun pocket. Overall German losses, including prisoners, were about 28,000. One of the victims was General Stemmermann, who was killed by artillery fire. For the Red Army commanders there were congratulations from Stalin: Konev was appointed a Marshal of the Soviet Union. For the Germans there was the bitter taste of defeat – tempered, perhaps, by the realisation that it had taken seven Soviet armies to deal with the six divisions they had bottled up in the wastes of the Korsun pocket.

ABOVE: The Belgian fascist leader Leon Degrelle (centre) who fought with the Wallonian Legion Brigade at Korsun. Degrelle was a great favourite of Adolf Hitler, and was often referred to as 'the son Hitler never had'. Degrelle avoided trial as a war criminal at the end of the war by flying to Spain.

The Taking of Pegasus Bridge

BELOW: Major John Howard, the leader of the paratroops who took and held the Orne bridges.

BELOW: Paras unload equipment, including a jeep, from a Horsa glider in Normandy.

Just before 11pm on the night of June 5 1944, only hours before the beginning of D-Day, the first of six Horsa gliders towed by Halifax bombers took off from Tarrant Rushton airfield in Dorset, southwest England. Their mission was to land the 150 men of D Company of the 2nd Oxfordshire and Buckinghamshire Light Infantry at the vital bridges on the River Orne and the adjacent Caen canal near the village of Benouville. The next morning – D-Day – would witness the biggest amphibious operation in history as the Allies attempted to wrest Europe from Germany's grasp.

The six Horsas were a small but crucial part of the huge airborne effort over Normandy which preceded the invasion and was designed to protect the flanks of the Allied beach-head and cut the lines of reinforcement to the German defenders of the target beaches.

The Ox and Bucks paratroops were comanded by Major John Howard, who had been given his orders, in great secrecy, on May 2. Considering the risks attendant on the operation, Major Howard calculated that at least half his force might not reach the bridges. Accordingly he planned to place one platoon and five engineers of his enlarged company into each of the six gliders. Each platoon would be trained to perform the task of all the others should the need arise.

While Howard's men set about their training, the glider pilots

were prepared for the operation, which was codenamed 'Deadstick'. The men of the Glider Pilot Regiment were trained to be 'Total Soldiers', capable of flying airborne troops into battle and then joining them on the ground, using whatever weapons were to hand. Part of their briefing was conducted by Flight Lieutenant Lawrence Wright, an artist and photographer who used a home-built forerunner of the modern computerised 'steadycam' special effects camera and a series of models to produce a film of the approach to the landing zones.

On May 28 the pilots were briefed by Howard, who hammered home the importance of landing as close as possible to the bridges. Meanwhile, the gliders were being modified for the mission, gaining an extra Perspex panel to give the pilot and co-pilot a better view, gyro compasses and arrester parachutes. The equipment with which they were carefully loaded included an assault boat, anti-tank rounds for the airborne troops' PIAT launchers and ammunition boxes. Now there was nothing left to do but wait.

On the night of June 5 the airfield at Tarrant Rushton was crowded with gliders – lines of the big tank-carrying Hamilcars ready for the next day and the six Horsas for Deadstick. At 11.30pm the first Halifax-glider combination, piloted by Staff Sergeants Wallwork and Ainsworth, rolled down the runway, bound for the bridge over the Orne canal, with the gliders piloted by Staff Sergeants Boland and Hobbs and Barkway and Boyle. The others, piloted by Staff Sergeants Lawrence and Shorter, Pearson and Guthrie and Howard and Baacke, were headed for the Orne river bridge.

The gliders were released over the French coast at 6,000ft (1,860m), leaving them to navigate to their landing zones by dead reckoning to make simultaneous landings at LZ Y (the Orne bridge) and LZ X (the Caen canal bridge). Shortly after midnight, Wallwork and Ainsworth picked out the river and canal shining in the moonlight. It was time for the final run-in and, behind the pilots, Howard's men linked arms and lifted their feet off the floor, bracing themselves for the crash-landing as the gliders swooped like huge kestrels towards their targets.

As the lead glider approached the canal bridge, the night was strangely silent. There was no firing. Then it made a rasping land-fall, showering sparks and, splintering like matchwood as it came to rest less than 50 yards (45m) away from the target, tossing the two pilots head-first through the shattered Perspex canopy into the barbed wire strung around the approach to the bridge. Behind them were the grinding sounds of the other gliders landing.

After narrowly avoiding a collision on the approach, Boland and Hobbs were the next in, surviving the landing almost intact. The third, piloted by Barkway and Boyle, landed at an angle, and came to a juddering halt on the edge of a pond, into which both its pilots were thrown. Stunned and half-drowned, they nevertheless clambered back to their wrecked glider, in which one man had been killed and several wounded, to begin unloading.

ABOVE: Two men of British 1st Airborne Division keep watch at a crossroads on the road to Caen three days after D-Day.

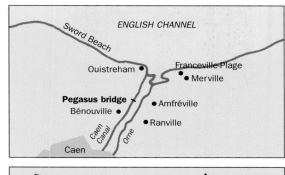

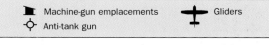

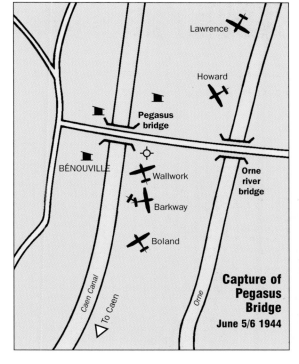

ABOVE: Commandos come ashore at D-Day on June 6. Lord Lovat's piper, whose bagpipes announced his arrival to relieve Pegasus Bridge, can be seen wading ashore in the centre of the picture.

BELOW: Aftermath of the taking of the Orne bridges: British infantry move on toward Caen.

As Major Howard clambered out of the wreckage of the first glider to land, he realised that he had achieved complete surprise. Some of the German defenders of the bridge knew nothing until they were rudely awoken by the crump of grenades. Others, groggily coming to, were confronted with the business end of a Sten gun.

Thirty men under Lieutenant Dan Brotheridge ran hell for leather for the opposite bank, where they could see a German sentry about to send up a flare. The sentry was cut down by automatic fire but not before the flare arced into the sky. Seconds later Brotheridge fell mortally wounded in the throat. No sooner had Brotheridge been shot than the survivors of Barkway's glider arrived, led by Lieutenant Sandy Smith who was nursing a badly broken arm. Smith and his men crossed to the far bank and within 15 minutes of landing the bridge had been taken.

The flare fired by the German sentry had been too late to warn the garrison holding the Orne river bridge. In one of the most remarkable feats of airmanship in the war, Sergeant Roy Howard had slithered through a herd of startled cows to bring his glider to within 6 yards (5.5m) of his objective. However, he was alone. One of his companions had come down several fields away while the other had landed 10 miles (16km) to the west at the wrong bridge. But the Orne bridge was taken without a shot being fired.

Ironically, neither of the bridges could have been blown, even if the Germans had been alerted during the gliders' approach. The British engineers discovered that, although some of the demolition

preparations had been completed, no explosive charges were in position. They were stored in a cottage nearby.

Howard's orders were to hold the bridge until relieved. In the pillbox covering the bridge, now cleared of its German occupants, Corporal Edward Tappendem was sending D-Day's first success signal – 'ham and jam ... ham and jam'. In the lull before the inevitable German counter-attack some of Howard's men knocked at the door of the tiny bar, owned by Monsieur Georges Gondree, beside the bridge. Gondree was reluctant to open up but when he heard British voices he threw open the doors, gave his unexpected customers a tearful welcome and began to uncork the bottles of champagne he had hidden for the liberation of France. It was 12.35pm and the first battle of D-Day was over.

Having gained their objectives, Howard's men beat off a succession of German counter-attacks launched by tanks, infantry and even a patrol boat despatched from Caen. At mid-day on June 6 they heard the wail of an approching bagpiper which signalled the arrival of the relieving force, Lord Lovat's Commandos, who had fought their way to the Orne bridges from the Normandy beach-head.

Within 48 hours the glider pilots were back in England. Barkway had been shot in the wrist while unloading his glider, a wound which was to cost him his arm. The men were all given leave. In London the next day Staff Sergeant Boyle was asked by an angry civilian why he wasn't fighting in France, to which he replied, 'I've been and come back.'

BACKGROUND PIC: American gliders in their drop zones on June 6 in another of the airborne operations launched as a preliminary to the assault on the five target beaches in Normandy.

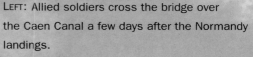

LEFT: Allied soldiers cross the bridge over the Caen Canal a few days after the Normandy landings.

Wittmann's Tank Battles

ABOVE: Michael Wittmann, the greatest tank ace of the war.

RIGHT: A column of Red Army T-34s on the move. Although these formidable tanks were Wittmann's principal opponents on the Eastern Front, the great tank ace claimed that enemy anti-tank guns were more prized targets.

World War II produced a host of fighter aces, a pack of U-boat aces and a number of less well-known figures — the tank aces. The most remarkable of these was the German tank commander Michael Wittmann, whose achievements were unsurpassed in the history of armoured warfare. Wittmann died as he lived, in Normandy in 1944, in one of the epic tank engagements of the war.

Wittmann was born in 1914 and joined the German Army as a private in 1934. In 1937 he joined the SS Leibstandarte, originally formed as Hitler's personal bodyguard, which was to expand into an armoured division in 1941. He served in Poland and France as an armoured car commander; in the Balkans, where he commanded an assault gun, he won the Iron Cross Second Class. Wittmann's meteoric rise began in the Russian campaign. During the battle for Rostov in the autumn of 1941 he destroyed six Red Army tanks in a single engagement. He then retrained as a tank commander with the rank of lieutenant and in 1943 was assigned a Tiger main battle tank in SS Panzer-Regiment I.

On the Eastern Front Wittmann became the archetypal tank ace. These armour-clad experten relied on the speed with which they read immediate tactical situations, a sixth sense for the unexpected movements of enemy vehicles, a coolness under attack which enabled them to hold their fire until the last possible moment and, perhaps most important of all, highly trained and experienced crews who were able to anticipate their commanders' orders. Above all, Wittmann possessed in Balthasar Woll a gunner who had an almost supernatural ability to fire accurately while on the move.

Wittmann's qualities were shown on the opening day of the battle of Kursk on July 5 1943, Hitler's doomed attempt to pinch off a huge salient jutting into the German battle line in the Ukraine. Spearheading the assault on the southern shoulder of the salient, Leibstandarte's armour advanced in a wedge formation with the Tigers of the division's heavy panzer company at the tip. Wittmann's platoon of five Tigers rolled forward. Woll targeted and destroyed his first Russian anti-tank gun of the day. The speed of the advance carried Wittmann's platoon on to an enemy strongpoint and a gaggle of T-34s, several of which were knocked out while the rest turned tail.

An hour later, as Wittmann took on another cluster of anti-tank guns, his radio crackled with the information that the company's Wendorff platoon had run into trouble. A swift change of direction plunged Wittmann's Tigers through a copse from which they emerged to find themselves in the rear of another enemy anti-tank strongpoint. In a nearby hollow, Wendorff's tanks were surrounded by T-34s which had set one of the Tigers on fire. Wittmann swung into action. Two of his tanks engaged the anti-tank guns while Wittmann went to the aid of Wendorff. Within five minutes he had knocked out three T-34s while sustaining serious damage to his own tank's tracks as the enemy returned fire. The advance was resumed and, by the end of the day, Wittmann had claimed eight enemy tanks knocked out and seven anti-tank guns destroyed.

Wittmann's tally on the Eastern Front had risen to 117 when, in January 1944, he was placed in command of 2 Company in the newly formed schwere (heavy) SS Panzer Abteilung 101. That summer, Wittmann was to wreak havoc on Allied armour in Normandy.

On June 12, six days after D-Day, the Allies were still fighting to secure their Normandy beach-head. The British 7th Armoured Division, veteran of tank battles in the Western Desert, was probing for a gap in the German line southwest of Caen. The landscape through which 7th Armoured was moving was known as the bocage, a jigsaw of small fields, orchards, thick hedgerows and sunken lanes – highly unsuitable terrain for armoured operations. At about 8am on the 13th, four Cromwell tanks of the Regimental Headquarters of the Fourth County of London Yeomanry, accompanied by infantry, occupied the village of Villers-Bocage, an important road centre, southwest of Caen. The Cromwells were part of 22nd Armoured Brigade, 7th Armoured's spearhead.

The gap for which they were aiming had hastily been closed by the three companies of Abteilung 101, rushed up from Beauvais under heavy air attack. Wittmann's company was concealed in woods northeast of Villers-Bocage, from which he emerged in his Tiger to conduct a personal reconnaissance. The first thing he saw was a British armoured column proceeding unconcernedly down the road to Villers-Bocage, outside of which it stopped for a 'brew-up'.

BELOW: End of a leviathan – a knocked-out Tiger in Normandy in the summer of 1944.

Eastern front, July 5 1943

ABOVE: Wittmann photographed in Belgium in the spring of 1944. Beside him is his legendary gunner Balthasar Woll.

TOP: The MkVI Tiger, which made its combat debut in Russia the summer of 1942. This formidable 55-ton beast, armed with an 88mm gun, won most of its battles but failed to influence the outcome of any campaign. In all, 1,350 were built.

Wittmann's Tiger then nosed its way into Villers-Bocage to discover the four Yeomanry Cromwells parked in the main street. He knocked out three of the tanks in quick succession, machine-gunning their crews as they raced for cover. The fourth, reversing at speed into a garden, escaped Wittmann's attentions and then began to stalk the Tiger.

Wittmann had reached the western outskirts of the village where he encountered another squadron of British tanks – four Sherman Fireflies armed with 17-pounder guns – waiting for orders to advance into Villers-Bocage. There was a short, sharp exchange of fire – in which one of the Fireflies hit Wittmann – before the Tiger withdrew, only to come face to face with the Cromwell which had been tailing him. The Cromwell's commander, Captain Pat Dyas, scored two direct but futile hits on Wittmann's massive frontal armour before a single shot from the Tiger's 88mm halted the Cromwell's charge. The crew scrambled out to be cut down by machine-gun fire. Only Dyas, who was wounded, managed to escape, to report the battle hotting up in Villers-Bocage.

Wittmann then huried back to his unit, which was still lurking in the woods, and proceeded to shoot up the British column halted outside the village. In less than ten minutes the British armoured spearhead had been reduced to a line of gutted hulks.

Meanwhile, three Cromwells and a Firefly of the Yeomanry's B Squadron had arrived by a roundabout route in the centre of the village, taking up position in side streets from which they hoped to ambush any Tigers pushing down the main road through Villers-Bocage.

Having rearmed and refuelled, Wittmann re-entered the rubble-strewn village with two Tigers and a MkIV panzer. He fell straight into the trap that had been set for him, sustaining a direct hit from a 6-pounder anti-tank gun brought in to support the Cromwells. Wittmann's left-side track flew off, sending the Tiger careering into a building while the following German tank blew up the house hiding the anti-tank weapon and its brave gunners. Then the Cromwells launched a co-ordinated attack, disabling the second Tiger with a single shot and placing a shell in the vulnerable engine compartment of the third. The German crews escaped on foot, leaving their tanks to be set ablaze.

Wittmann's company had inflicted 100 casualties and destroyed 20 Cromwells, four Fireflies, three light tanks, three scout cars and a half-track. As night fell, the British pulled back. The Germans rushed in reinforcements, including units from 2nd Panzer Division and a task force detached from the Panzer Lehr Division, to secure Villers-Bocage which was subsequently levelled by Allied bombers.

Wittmann did not long survive his triumph at Villers-Bocage, for which he was awarded the Swords to his Knight's Cross and promoted to the command of Abteilung 101. On August 9, in fighting on the Caen-Falaise road, the tank ace was ambushed by a Firefly of the British 1st Northamptonshire Yeomanry which blew his Tiger apart at virtually point blank range. Wittmann's body lay buried at the side of the road until 1983, when it was reinterred in a German war cemetery at La Cambe. His final victory tally, achieved in less than three years, stood at 138 tanks and assault guns and 132 anti-tank guns.

ABOVE: The Knight's Cross of the Iron Cross with oak leaves and sword, the honour with which Wittmann was awarded.

BELOW: Wittmann, under the muzzle break of his Tiger's 88mm gun, and Woll, pictured on the Eastern Front at a time when the ace and his crew had destroyed 88 Red Army tanks.

The Doolittle Raid

ABOVE: Colonel James Doolittle (standing, left) with Admiral Marc A. Mitscher on the deck of the carrier *Hornet* just before the raid on Tokyo.

BELOW: A B-25 staggers off the heaving deck of *Hornet*, watched anxiously by crew of the carrier. The bomber crews were not confident of their safe return.

It did not take long for the Americans to recover from the Japanese attack on Pearl Harbor on December 7 1941. Four months after the devastating strike against the home of the US Pacific Fleet the Japanese were still running riot in the Pacific, capturing Manila in the Philippines, occupying Java and driving the British out of Rangoon, the capital of Burma. But amid a strategic picture of intense gloom, the foundations were being laid for Allied victory in the Pacific.

On March 10 1942, in a foretaste of things to come, 100 aircraft from the US carriers *Lexington* and *Yorktown*, positioned in the Coral Sea, had attacked Japanese transports off the coast of New Guinea. In what was the biggest American air strike thus far in the war, they sank four Japanese ships and damaged five others. Five weeks later the US Pacific Fleet was to mount an operation which confirmed the worst fears of the Japanese High Command – an attack by American carrier-borne planes on the Japanese home islands.

The raid was planned by General H. 'Hap' Arnold, chief of the US Army Air Forces, and was to be led by the 46-year-old Colonel James H. Doolittle, who had flown with the US Army Air Corps in World War I and subsequently gained a daredevil reputation as a racing and publicity pilot, scooping long-distance flying trophies and setting many records.

The raid was to be flown by USAAF Mitchell B-25 medium bombers. The Mitchell had been named in honour of the controversial US Army Air Corps officer who was court-martialled in 1924 for his passionate advocacy of air power. Eventually the B-25 was made in greater quantity than any other twin-engined American combat aircraft, but it had not been designed to fly from carriers. The mission which Doolittle was to lead was to be hazardous from the very moment of take-off.

Only 16 Mitchells were to fly against Japan, each one stripped of all extraneous equipment and most of its armament. As many as 10,000 personnel were involved in the preparation and execution of the strike, from high-ranking air planners to the technicians at Wright Field, Eglin and Sacramento who prepared the B-25s and the crews of the naval task force which was to launch the attack. The Mitchells were embarked on the carrier *Hornet*, accompanied by the carrier *Enterprise*. These carriers, which had escaped destruction at Pearl Harbor, were to be in the vanguard of the

American fightback in the Pacific. Overall command of the operation lay in the hands of Admiral William E. 'Bull' Halsey, sailing in the *Enterprise*.

It was only when *Hornet* was 24 hours out of San Francisco that Doolittle revealed the details of the mission to the men under his command. In his characteristically laconic style, he told them that they were going to attack Tokyo, Yokohama, Osaka, Kobe and Nagoya. After hitting their targets, the Mitchells would fly on to China where they would land at small airfields near the coast, refuel and then proceed to Chungking, the capital of the Chinese Nationalist leader Chiang-Kai-shek. (The original plan had been to fly on to Vladivostok in the Soviet Union, but the Russians, who were not at war with the Japanese, had turned down the proposal.)

Doolittle warned the aircrew tasked with attacking Tokyo that, on no account, were they to bomb the Emperor's palace, the so-called 'Temple of Heaven'. Doolittle knew from his own experiences in the London 'Blitz', when Buckingham Palace was hit, that any attack on the Emperor would only stiffen Japanese morale. Aboard the *Hornet* were two US Navy officers who had a detailed knowledge of the targets chosen for the mission. Veterans of postings in Japan, they gave the crews intensive briefings on target identification and even taught them some basic Chinese, to use if they had to bale out over China.

Doolittle had originally planned to take off at about 4pm on the afternoon of April 18. This would ensure that he arrived over Tokyo just before nightfall to illuminate his targets with 2,000lb (900kg) of incendiary bombs. The remaining 15 planes would take off from *Hornet* just before dusk, to reach their targets under the cover of darkness. Japanese night fighter defences were, at this stage in the war, virtually non-existent. The B-25s would attack from 1,500ft (450m), above the range of light anti-aircraft defences but well below that of the heavier pieces' calibration. The plan of attack would also bring the Mitchells over the Chinese coast at dawn, when they could more readily spot their landing fields.

But early on the morning of April 18, Doolittle's plan was wrecked when *Hornet* was spotted by a Japanese patrol ship some 830 miles (1330km) off the Japanese coast. The patrol ship was speedily sunk but it was almost certain that it had radioed the position of the task force to the Japanese high command. Halsey had no alternative but to order an immediate take-off at a longer range than had been planned.

Now came a supreme test of airmanship. The pitching of the *Hornet* in a heavy sea forced the B-25s to adopt a drastic take-off manoeuvre. The only way of getting airborne was to wait until the bow reached its lowest

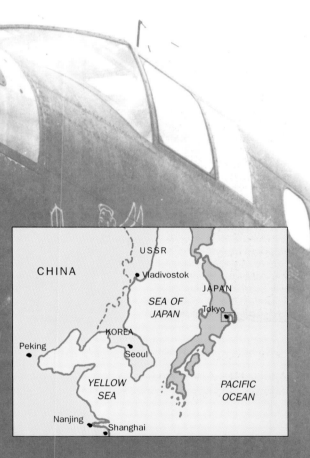

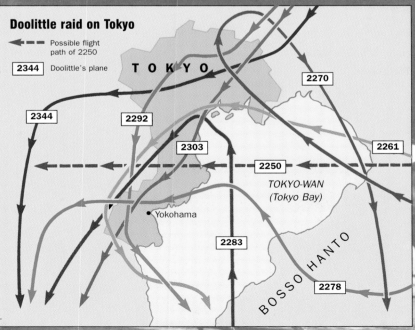

Doolittle raid on Tokyo

◄--- Possible flight path of 2250

2344 Doolittle's plane

TOKYO

2344 2292 2270 2303 2261 2250

TOKYO-WAN (Tokyo Bay)

Yokohama

2283 2278

BOSSO HANTO

point, dipping into the sea, and then, as it came up, to launch each B-25. The Mitchells would have the brief advantage – some two seconds – of travelling downhill and, if they had calculated correctly, would reach the end of the flight deck when the nose of the carrier was just about level.

Doolittle gave his men a final instruction. The long voyage on *Hornet* had affected the B-25s' compasses. As each plane took off, it was to circle and then fly directly along the length of the carrier, which was heading due west, to realign the compass. As each man clambered into his bomber, he was given a bottle of whisky.

Doolittle was the first to take off. With full flaps and engine roaring at maximum throttle, his B-25 plunged down the flight deck into the teeth of a 27-knot gale. As *Hornet* rose into a level position, Doolittle took off with 100ft (30m) to spare, hanging the B-25 almost straight up on its props, levelling off and coming round in a tight circle. One by one, the remaining 15 B-25s struggled into the air. Doolittle headed for Tokyo, flying at a height of barely 200ft (60m). As he crossed the Japanese coast five hours later, he was joined by the B-25 flown by Lieutenant Travis Hoover. The two bombers dipped wings in greeting.

The B-25s had made landfall about 30 miles (50km) from Tokyo, but as they flew south at treetop height, their olive drab colour scheme blending with the forest below, they were confronted with five enemy fighters dead ahead and flying at 1,500ft (450m). Doolittle and Hoover jinked through a valley and managed to throw off their pursuers, who disappeared to the east.

Over Tokyo, Doolittle released his incendiaries amid a storm of anti-aircraft fire. One shell, bursting very close to him, peppered his B-25 with metal fragments. Doolittle took his plane down to 100ft (30m), studiously

BELOW: Mission perilous. Doolittle's raiders lined up on *Hornet*, with another of the 16-ship task force in the background.

ignoring the chance to strafe targets of opportunity, which would only have raised hell for those planes flying in after him.

As Doolittle crossed the Chinese coast, he searched for a homing fix from an American aircraft flown for that purpose from Chungking to Chu Chow. What he did not know was that this airborne beacon had crashed near Chu Chow, killing all its crew. His pleas for a fix from Chinese radio operators below were greeted with silence. The Chinese, unaware of the raid, were convinced that it was a Japanese ruse and had ordered a total radio silence.

Climbing to 9,000ft (2,750m), Doolittle began to search for Chu Chow, which lay in a valley surrounded by 4,000ft (1,200m) mountains. But darkness and foul weather had now closed in. Soon his fuel gauge read empty. Doolittle put the plane on auto-pilot and then he and his crew baled out into the night. Doolittle himself made a soft landing in a paddy field.

Not one of the aircraft under Doolittle's command landed safely in China. One of the Mitchells reached the forbidden haven of Valdivostok, where its crew were interned. Like Doolittle, the others crashed when they ran out of fuel. Doolittle and 62 of his men survived after parachuting over China. Four drowned and one was killed after baling out. The Japanese captured eight of Doolittle's men and executed three of them for committing 'inhuman acts'. Another died in a prison camp. In the end, 71 of these brave airmen survived the war.

The B-25s had caused little or no serious damage, but had nevertheless delivered a massive psychological blow to the Japanese, who immediately accelerated their plans for a showdown with the US Pacific Fleet which were to end in defeat at the Battle of Midway, one of the key turning points of the war. For his part in the raid, Doolittle was promoted to the rank of Brigadier-General and awarded the Medal of Honor. He finished a distinguished wartime career in command of 8th Air Force in the Pacific, helping to seal the fate of Japan in a series of shattering raids on her blazing cities. Doolittle, one of the great airmen of the war, had been one of the first and the last.

ABOVE: Landfall over Japan. A Japanese naval base photographed from the nose of one of Doolittle's B-25s.

TOP: Friendly flight: a B-25 cruises over Castle air force base in California with the remarkable Doolittle at the controls.

Index

Figures in **bold** type represent references in captions to illustrations

A

Aachen, 12
Achates, HMS, 52
Admiral Hipper, 51, 52, **52**
Afrika Korps (German), 34
Ainsworth, Staff Sgt, 99
Air Intelligence (British), 15
Airborne troops, German, 63
Aitken, Sub-Lt, **73**
Albergo-Rifugia Hotel, **62**
Albert Canal, 10
Alexander, Gen Sir Harold, 75
Alexander, Lt Col Leigh, 67
Allied Forces Southwest Pacific, 30
American Volunteer Group (AVG), 68
Amilakvari, Lt-Col, 34
Anders, Gen Wladyslaw, 77
Anzio, 74
Arakan, 82
Ardennes, 10
Armstrong-Whitworth Whitley, 15, **16**
Arnold, Gen H. 'Hap', 106
Arzew, 86
Assam, 82
Assault Group Koch (German), 11
Assault Section Granite (German), **10**, 11
Avro Lancaster, 22–

B

Baacke, Staff Sgt, 99
Ballale, 19
Bangkok, 8
Barents Sea, Battle of, 50–
Barkway, Staff Sgt, 99
Bataan Pensinsula, 30
Bataan Pensinsula, 43
Belgium, 10
Ben My Chree, USS, 47
Benouville, 98
Bir Hacheim, 34–
Bismarck Sea, Battle of, 43
'Black Sheep' (VMF-214), 18
Black Watch regiment, 15
Blackett Strait, 44
Boland, Staff Sgt, 99
Bougainville, 19, 44
'Bouncing bomb', 22, 25
Boyington, Major Gregory 'Pappy', 18, 19, 20, 21, **21**
Boyle, Staff Sgt, 99
Bramble, HMS, 52
British Army 1st Airborne Division, 99
  2nd Oxfordshire and Buckinghamshsire Light Infantry, 98–
  77th Indian Infantry Brigade ('Chindits'), 66–
  7th Armoured Division, 103
  Eighth Army, 75
  GHQ Liaison Regiment, 59
  IV Corps, 68
  XXXIII Corps, 83
  10th Gurkha Rifles, **84**
  14th Army, 82
Brotheridge, Lt Dan, 100
Bruneval raid, 14–

Bulkeley, Lt Commander John, 42
Bull Basket, Operation, **61**
Burma Road, 7
Burma, 7, 66–, 82. 106
Burnett, Rear Admiral, 51

C

Caen Canal bridge, 99
Caen, 103
Calvario, Mount, 76
Calvert, Maj Michael 'Mad Mike', 68
Cameron, Lt Donald, **70**–
Cape Torokina, **21**
Central Aircraft Manufacturing Co (CAMCO), 7
Cephalonia, 91
Charteris, Lt Euen, 56
Chartres, 59
Chastise, Operation, 24
Chennault, Claire, 6, **6**, **98**
Cherkassy, 94–
Chiang Kai-shek, 6, 107
China Air Task Force, 9
Chinchar, Sgt Mike, 40
Chindits, 66–
Chindwin River, 67
Chinese Air Force, 6
Chu Chow, 109
Chungking, 107
Cisterna, 89
Clark, Lt-Gen Mark, 74
Clifford, Lt E. W., 92, **92**
Coastwatchers, 45
Cologne, 38
Cologne-Ostheim airfield, 11
Conte di Cavour, 92
Convoy JW51A, 51
Convoy JW51B, 51
Convoy PQ-17, 50
Cooke, Lt-Col S., 67
Corregidor, 30–
Cox, Flight Sgt C.W.H.5, 16
Cromwell tanks, 103
Cunningham, Admiral Sir Andrew, 90–
Cunningham, Commander W. Scott, 78–
Curtiss Hawk 75 Special, 6
Curtiss-Wright P-40 Tomahawk, 6, 7, 8

D

Dam Busters, 22–
Dammer, Major Herman W., 87
Darby, Col William, **86**–
Davidson, Lt, 80
D-Day, 46–, 59, 98, 103
Deadstick, Operation, 99
Degrelle, Leon, **97**
Delisio, Sgt Joseph, 39
Devereaux, Major James P., 79
DFS 230 glider, 13
Dijon-Paris rail line, 59
Dimapur, 82
Dnieper, 95
Donitz, Admiral Karl, 26–
Doolittle, Col James H., 106–
Douglas C-47 Dakota, 31, 32, **68**
Douglas C-47, 31, 32
Drabika, Sgt Alex, 41
Duilio, 92

Dyas, Capt Pat, 104

E

Eagle, HMS, 91
Eben Emael, 10–
Eder dam, 22, 24, **24**, 25
Eighth Army (British), 34
Elrod, Capt Henry, 80
Engeman, Lt-Col Leonard, 39
Ennepe dam, 25
Enterprise, USS, 106–
Ethiopia, 66
Etterlin, Gen Frtido von Senger und, 75
Evans, Lt A.R., 45
Ewing, Capt Robert T., 19

F

Fairey Swordfish, 90–
Faust, Sgt, 41
Fergusson, Maj-Gen, 67, 68
Fieseler Storch, **63**, 64
Flying Tigers, 6–8,
Fort Mills, 30
Franklin, USS, 21
Free French Brigade, First, 34–
Freyburg, Gen Sir Bernard, 76
Friedrich Eckholdt, 53
Friesenhann, Capt Karl, 40
Frost, Major John, 15, **17**

G

Gafsa, 87–
'Gain', Operation, 59
Garigliano River, 74
Garrison Hill, 83–
Gazala Line, 34
Gerlach, Cap, 65
German Army
  10th Army, 74
  1st Parachute Division, 75
  90th Light Division, 35
  Afrika Korps, 88
  Belgian SS Wallonian Brigade, 95
  Coastal Artillery Regiment 1260, 47
  Group B, 39
  Group South, 94
  Infantry Regiment 726, 47
  SS Leibstandarte, 102
  SS Panzer Abteilung 101, 103
  SS Panzer Division Wiking, 94–
  Volkssturm, 39
Gestapo, 60
Gibson, Sqn Ldr Guy, 22, 23, 24, **24**, 25
Gideon Force, 66
Gniloy Tich River, 97
Gondree, Monsieur Georges, 101
Graf Zeppelin, 53
Gran Sasso, 62–
'Grand Slam' bomb, 25
Grimball, Lt John, 39
Grumman F4F Wildcat, **78**–
Guadalcanal, 18, 43
Guam, 78
Gurkhas, 67
Gustav Line, 74
Guthrie, Staff Sgt, 99

H

Hale, Lt-Commander 'Ginger', 91
Halsey, Admiral William E. 'Bull', 107
Handley Page Halifax, 98
Harris, Air Marshal, 22
Hawaii, 78
Hawker Hurricane, 36
Hayate, 80
Hedman, Bob 'Duke', 8
Heinkel He 111, 63,
Henty-Creer, Lt, 73
Hildesheim, 11
Hill, Sqn Ldr A.E., **14**
Hiryu, 81
Hislop, Capt John, 60
Hitler, Adolf, 10, 11, 26, 62, **65**
Hitzfield, Major-General, 40
Hobbs, Staff Sgt, 99
Hoover, Lt Travis, 108
Hopgood, Flt Lt, 24
Hornet, USS, **44**, 106–
Horsa gliders, 98–
Howard, Major John, **98–**
Howard, Staff Sgt, 99

I

Illustrious, HMS, 90–
Imphal, 82–
Irrawaddy River, 68
Itagaki, Capt Agira, 31
Italian Army 101st Armoured Division, 35
  102nd Ariete Division, 35
  Bersaglieri, 86
  Trieste Division, 35
Italian Navy, 90–
Iwo Jima, 54–

J

Jamaica, HMS, 51, 53
Japanese 15th Army, 82
Japanese Air Force, 6
Japanese Marines, 81
Jez, Private First Class Leo, 55
Jones, Col George M., 31, 32
Jones, Dr R. V., 14
Jottrand, Major, 12
Judgement, Operation, 90
Juin, Gen Alphonse, 77
Junkers Ju 87 Stuka, 36, 37

K

Kaafjord, 70
Kahili, 19
Kajioka, Admiral, 80
Kennedy, Lt John F., 44–
Kesselring, Field Marshal Albert, 74
King's Own Scottish Borderers regiment, 15
Kinloch, Lt David, 52
Kisaragi, 80
Kobe, 107
Koenig, General Marie-Pierre, 34–
Kohima, 82–
Kolombangara, 45
Konev, Gen, 94
Korean War, 21
Korsun-Cherkassy, 94–
Kravchenko, Gen, 94
Kriegsmarine, 26
Kummetz, Vice-Admiral Oscar, 52
Kunming, 6
Kuomintang, 6
Kuribyashi, Lt-Gen Todomichi, 54
Kursk, Battle of , 102

L

La Cambe, 105

Lamb, Lt Charles, 92
Lawrence, Staff Sgt, 99
Le Havre, 15
Lea, Lt C. S. C., 92
Lentaigne, Brig William 'Joe', 69
Lexington, USS, 106
Leyte Island, 30
Liri Valley, 74
Littorio, 92
Liversedge, Col Harry B. 'Harry the Horse', 55, 57
Long Range Desert Group, British, 58
Lovatt, Lord, **100**
Low Countries, 10
'Loyton', Operation, 60
Luck (Royal Navy crewman), **73**
Ludendorff railway bridge, 38–
Lutzow, 51
Lutzow, 71
Luzon, 30
Lyster, Admiral, 93
Lysyanka, 96

M

Maas River, 10
MacArthur, General Douglas, 30, 43
Magennis (Royal Navy rating), **73**
Maginot Line, 10
Magwe, 9
Malaya, HMS, 91
Mandalay-Myitkyina railway, 67
Manila Bay, 30
Manila, 30, 106
Marianas, 54
Martin, Mickey, 22
Martino, Chief Torpedoman, 43
Maund, Lt M.R., 92
Mayne, Lt-Col R.B. 'Paddy', **59**
McCarter, Private Lloyd, 32
McCarthy, Flt Lt Joe, 23, 25
McDonnell Douglas A-4 Skyhawk, 21
McMahon, Patrick, 44
Mindanao, 43
Mindoro, 30
Mingladon, 8
Mitchell, Major-General Ralph J., 18
Mitscher, Admiral Marc A., **106**
Mitsubishi A6M Zero, 7, 19, 20, 21
Model, Field Marshal Walther, 39
Moehne dam, 22, **23**, 24, 25
Monte Cassino, 74–
Moshny, 95
Mountbatten, Admiral Lord Louis, 15, 69
Moussey, 60
Munda, 19,
Munda, 44,
Murmansk, 51,
Mussolini, Benito ('Il Duce'), 62–
Mutaguchi, Gen Renya, 82–

N

Nagoya, 107
Nancy, 60
New Georgia Island, 19, 44
New Guinea, 30
New Guinea, 44
Nimitz, Admiral, 57
Normandy, 59, 98, 103
North Africa, 34, 58
North American B-25 Mitchell, 9, 106
North Cape, 50
Norway campaign, 12

O

Oahu, 78
Obdurate, HMS, 52

Obedient, HMS, 52
Okinawa, 54
Omaha Beach, 46
Onslow, HMS, 50–
Orkneys, 27
Orne River, 98–
Orwell, HMS, 52
Osaka, 107
Overlord, **58**, 59

P

Patrol Torpedo Boats (PT-boats), 42–
Pearl Harbor, 7, 78, 93
Pearson, Staff Sgt, 99
Pegasus Bridge, 98–
Pegasus, HMS, 27
Pershing M-26 tanks, 38
Pescara, 74
Philip, Lt Peter, **73**
Philippines, 30, 42, 54, 78, 106
Pickard, Sqn Ldr Charles, **14**, 15
Place, Lt B. C. G., **70–**
Place, Lt Godfrey, 72
Pointe du Hoc, 46–
Pound, Admiral Sir Dudley, 90
Prien, Gunther, 27–
PT-109, 44, 45, **45**
PT-34, 42, 43
PT-38, **43**
PT-463, **42**
PT-boats, 31
PT-boats, 42–
Putnam, Major Paul A., 79
Pye, Admiral William, 81

R

Rabaul, 18, 20
RAF 617 Squadron, 22–
RAF Bomber Command, 22
RAF Desert Air Force, 37
RAF Fighter Command 14
RAF Photographic Interpretation Unit, 15
Rambouillet, 59
Ramillies, HMS, 91
Rangoon, 7, 106
Rapido, 74
Rastenburg, 62
Red Army, 94–
Remagen, 38–
Repulse, HMS, 27
Resistance, French, 15, 48, **58**, 59, **60**
Rhine, River, 38–
Ribbentropp, Joachim, von, 60
Richards, Col Hugh, 83
Rome, 63
Rome, 74
Rommel, Field Marshal Erwin, 34
Ronda Segnali, 35
Rosenthal, Joe, 54, 56
Ross, George, 45
Ross, Lt John, 15
Rotmistrov, Gen Pavel, 94
Rouen, 59
Royal Air Force, 7
Royal Navy 12th Submarine Flotilla, 70
Royal Navy Fleet Air Arm, 91
Royal Navy, 15, 26
Royal New Zealand Air Force, 18
Royal Oak, HMS, 26–
Rudder, Lt-Colonel, 46–
Rurh industrial region, 22
Russell Islands, 19
Russian Army, 94–

S

Salween Gorge, 9

Saratoga, USS, 81
Sato, General, 83
Scapa Flow, 26–
Scarlett, Lt N.J. Blood, 92
Scharnhorst, 71
Scheller, Hans, 40
Schmidt, Maj-Gen, Harry, 54
Scoones, Lt-Gen, 68
Scraggy Hill, **84**
Seaforths regiment, 15
Seanymph, HMS, 71
Sened Pass, 86–
Sfax, 87
Sheffield, HMS, 50–
Sherbrooke, Capt Robert, 50–
Sherman Firefly tanks, 104
Sherrod, Robert, 57
Shorter, Staff Sgt, 99
Siam, Gulf of, 8
Sixth Army (German), 12
Skorzeny, Capt Otto, **62**–
Slim, Gen William, 82
Smith, R.T. 'Tadpole', 8
Soletti, General, 63
Solomon Islands, 43, 78
Solomons Campaign, 18
Soroy Island, 71
Sorpe dam, 22, 24, 25
Soryu, 80
'Source' Operation, 70–
Special Air Service (SAS), British, 58–
Special Night Squads, British, 66
Spitzbergen, **72**
SS, German, 60
Stemmermann, Gen, 96
Sterling, Captain David, 58
Stibbe, Lt Philip, 68
Stilwell, Gen 'Vinegar Joe', 9, 69
Stopford, Lt-Gen Montagu, 83
Stubborn, HMS 71
Student, General Kurt, 63, 12
Subic Bay, 42
Supermarine Spitfire, **14**, 17, 70
Suribachi, Mount, 54, 55, 56
Swayne, Lt H.I., 91
Syrtis, HMS, 71

T
T-34 tank, **94**, **102**
'Tallboy' bomb, 25
Taranto, 90–

Task Force Engemann, 38
Texas, USS, 47
Tiger tanks, 102–
Timmermann, Lt Karl, 38–
Timothy, Lt John, 15
Tirpitz, 25, 70
Tobruk, 34
Tokyo, 107–
'Tokyo Express', 43, 44, 45
Torch landings, 51
Torch, Operation, 86
Toungoo, 7
Travers, Susan, 37
Trento, 93
Truscott, Gen Lucien, **47**, **89**
Tulagi, 43
Tunisia, 86–

U
U-16, 26
U-47 26–
U-boats, 26–, 50
U-go offensive, 69, 82
Ukraine, 102
United States Army Air Force (USAAF), 9
  9th Air Force, 46
  14th Air Force, 8, 9
  Air Commando, 68, 69
US Army
  1st Army, 38–
  27th Armored Infantry Batalion, 38–
  2nd Ranger Battalion, 46–
  34th Infantry Regiment, 32
  503rd Parachute Regiment, 30–
  5th Rangers, 49
  9th Armored Division, 38
  Fifth Army, 75
  Sixth Army, 30
  Rangers, 46–, 86–
  Third Army, 60
  V Corps, 46
  VII Corps, 46
US Marine Corps, 18, 54, 78
US Marines Fighter Squadron 214 (VMF-214), 18, 21
US Navy, 18
Utah Beach, 46

V
V-2 rocket, **39**
Vaenga, 70

Valiant, HMS, 91
Vatutin, Gen, 94
Vella Lavella, 20, 44
Vierville, 49
Vietnam War, 21
Vila, 44
Villers-Bocage, 103
Vladivostok, 107
Vosges, 60
Vought F4U Corsair, **18**, 19, 20, **20**

W
Waffen-SS, 62
Wainwright, General, 30
Wake Island, 78–
Wallis, Barnes, 22–
Wallwork, Staff Sgt, 99
Warspite, HMS, 91
Welham, Lt J. W. G., 92
Wenzel, Sergeant-Major Helmut, 12
Western Desert, 34
Whiteley (Royal Navy Artificer), **73**
Whittam, Sub-Lt, 73
Williamson, Lt-Commander K. 'Hooch', 91, 92
Wingate, Maj-Gen Orde, **66**
Wittmann, Michael, **102**–
Witzig, Lieutenant Rudolf, 11
Woll, Balthasar, 102–
Wright, Flt Lt, Lawrence, 99
Wurzburg radar installation, 14, **14**

X
X-craft:
  X-10, 71–
  X-3, 70
  X-4, 70
  X-5, 71–
  X-6, 71–
  X-7, 71–
  X-8, 71–
  X-9, 71–

Y
Yamamoto, Admiral, 93
Yokohama, 107
Yorktown, USS, 106
Yubari, 80
Yunnan province, 6, 8

Picture Credits

Jacket: front, MEL; back, main pic IWM, top left IWM via TRH Pictures (TRH), bottom IWM. Page 1,via Peter Newarkís Military Pictures (Peter Newark); 3, via MEL; 5, via MEL; 6, via MEL; 7, via Robert Hunt Library; 8-9, top left via MEL, background pic and top right via Robert Hunt Library; 10, top, via Robert Hunt Library, bottom via MEL; 12, top via MEL, bottom via Peter Newark; 13, via Bruce Robertson; 14, via TRH; 16, background pic, via Bruce Robertson, top left IWM, top right and bottom right IWM via TRH; 18-19, Corbis-Bettmann/UPI; 20-21, background pic via TRH, others Corbis-Bettmann/UPI; 23, top via Peter Newark, bottom via Bruce Robertson; 24, top Robert Hunt Library, bottom, via MEL; 25, RAF Museum via TRH; 26, via TRH; 27, Robert Hunt Library; 28-29, left via Peter Newark, bottom via TRH, top via Robert Hunt Library; 31, US National Archives via TRH; 32-33, US National Archives via TRH; 34, via TRH; 35, top via Robert Hunt Library, bottom, IWM; 36, via Peter Newark; 37, top via Robert Hunt Library, bottom IWM; 38-39, via Peter Newark; 40, top via Peter Newark, bottom via Robert Hunt Library; 41, via Robert Hunt Library; 42-43, via TRH; 44, via TRH; 45, top Popperfoto, bottom via Peter Newark; 46, Popperfoto; 47, background pic, IWM, inset via Peter Newark; 48-49, left Robert Hunt Library, centre Popperfoto, right IWM via TRH; 50-51, IWM; 52, top IWM, bottom, via TRH; 53, IWM; 54-55, top via Peter Newark; bottom, USMC via TRH, right US Navy via TRH; 56, US National Archives via TRH; 57, top via Peter Newark, bottom USMC via TRH; 58-59, via Peter Newark; 60 Popperfoto; 61, IWM via TRH; 62-63, via Peter Newark; 64-65, via Peter Newark; 66-67, via MEL; 68-69, Via MEL; 70-71, Popperfoto; 72-73, left and centre Robert Hunt Library, top right via MEL, bottom right Popperfoto; 74-75, via MEL; 76-77, background pic and bottom left, IWM via TRH, others via MEL; 80-81, background pic via Bruce Robertson, inset via Topham Picturepoint; 80, Topham Picturepoint; 81, top Robert Hunt Library, bottom, Tophamd Picturepoint; 82, IWM; 83, top IWM, bottom Robert Hunt Library; 84, IWM; 85, top Robert Hunt Library, bottom IWM; 86, US National Archives via TRH; 87, top Popperfoto, bottom IWM via TRH; 88, top via TRH , bottom Popperfoto; 89, via MEL; 90, top via Peter Newark, bottom via Bruce Robertson; 92, top US Navy via TRH, bottom Fleet Air Arm via TRH; 93, top Popperfoto, bottom via Bruce Robertson; 94, via TRH; 95, ESP via TRH; 96-97, top left and top right via TRH, bottom ESP via TRH; 98, via MEL; 99, IWM; 100-101, background pic via MEL, top left IWM via TRH, bottom left Popperfoto, right IWM; 102, BDC via Bruce Quarrie; 103, top Topham , bottom via MEL; 104, top via TRH, bottom Archiv Ott-Gettorf via Bruce Quarrie; 105, top via Peter Newark, bottom via TRH; 106-107 via MEL; 108-109, via MEL.